ST. THOMAS BECKET IN ART

PLATE I

STATUES IN EASTERN APSIDAL CHAPEL, HENRY VII's CHAPEL,
WESTMINSTER ABBEY

EARLY SIXTEENTH CENTURY

ST. THOMAS BECKET
IN ART

BY

TANCRED BORENIUS, Ph.D., D.Lit.

DURNING-LAWRENCE PROFESSOR OF THE HISTORY
OF ART IN THE UNIVERSITY OF LONDON

WITH FORTY-FOUR PLATES
AND FIVE ILLUSTRATIONS IN THE TEXT

KENNIKAT PRESS
Port Washington, N. Y./London

ST. THOMAS BECKET IN ART

First published in 1932
Reissued in 1970 by Kennikat Press
Library of Congress Catalog Card No: 70-102835
SBN 8046-0750-8

Manufactured by Taylor Publishing Company   Dallas, Texas

1990945

PREFACE

THE first Englishman, so far as I am aware, to mention Vittore Carpaccio, Edward Wright, who visited Italy in 1720–22, remarks *à propos* of the since so famous series of pictures of the life of St. Ursula: " We meet sometimes in Italy with memorials of Kings of England which we find no mention made of in our chronicles." However that may be, there is one absolutely authentic and tangible character in English mediæval history of whom numerous memorials may be found to this day not only in Italy but all over the Continent as well as in England—memorials which originally were even more numerous and covered an even wider area : namely, St. Thomas Becket. The martyred Archbishop represents indeed England's principal contribution—and a highly important one—to mediæval iconography : the drama of his life stirred public imagination in the twelfth century even more profoundly than, for instance, the humiliation and penance of Henry IV at Canossa in the preceding century : and the enormous proportions eventually assumed by the pilgrimages to his tomb and the countless miracles which his devotees would point to as having been worked through his intercession, combined to give to the cult of St. Thomas an outstanding importance. In London the veneration for the Saint, who was a native of the city, was particularly intense down to the year 1538 when an abrupt and violent break was made with tradition : indeed one may say that by then St. Thomas Becket had come to be regarded as being, in effect, the patron saint of London.

Some day, perhaps, a book will be written dealing exhaustively with the subject of the cult of St. Thomas Becket from all its aspects : and there can be no doubt that it would be a most important contribution towards the study and interpretation of mediæval civilization. Meanwhile, I have thought it worth while to try and piece together the available information concerning the representation of St. Thomas Becket in art. It will be seen that it is an enquiry which takes us into many countries and across many centuries : we can also gauge from this material with what eagerness the mediæval artist availed himself of the chances offered by a subject-matter so near to him in time ; while it is of peculiar interest to observe how the different countries and periods of art, each in their way, condition the representation of St. Thomas.

To me personally, the preoccupation with St. Thomas Becket has provided an intellectual companionship extending over several years. Merely to attempt to visualize the varied episodes of the eventful life of the proud Norman, in whom the warrior was but insufficiently merged in the archbishop—with the scene shifting to and from Canterbury and the fields and villages of Kent, the woods of Wiltshire, storm-tossed Channel passages, fair cities of France, whose very names are full of evocative power and many other settings impossible to particularize—merely to attempt to visualize all this, has been an experience of enormous fascination. And then there has been the immense interest of the quest for the widely scattered material, never yet adequately surveyed, showing how that character and that life were reflected in art.

In carrying out this task, I have laid myself under an indebtedness to so many quarters that it is not easy to give an adequate expression to my obligations. I am particularly indebted to the Society of Antiquaries,

which has accorded the hospitality of its annual *Archæologia* (Vols. LXXIX and LXXXI) to two of my pre-
liminary papers on the subject, and has also kindly
allowed me to use in this volume the blocks made for
the illustrations of those papers. I further owe a heavy
debt of gratitude to the Rev. George Herbert, who has
collected a number of very valuable notes on the subject of my study and most generously has placed them
at my disposal. For various friendly offices I should,
moreover, like here to thank the Rev. E. E. Dorling,
F.S.A., Dr. Joan Evans, Dr. Giuseppe Gerola, Don
Manuel Gómez-Moreno, Dr. Walter L. Hildburgh,
F.S.A., Mr Hedley Hope-Nicholson, Mr. Philip M.
Johnston, F.S.A., Herr F. A. Martens, Professor Andrea
Moschetti, Dr. Philip Nelson, F.S.A., Dr. Nikolaus
Pevsner, Professor Wolfgang Stammler, Mr. W. Frederick
Stohlman and Mr. Francis Wormald. No one can ever
hope to carry out an enquiry of the nature here involved
without assistance from a great many quarters ; and I
am deeply conscious of the kindness and help I have
experienced in so large a measure.

T. B.

STOCKS BRIDGE COTTAGE,
    COOMBE BISSETT, WILTSHIRE.
St. Thomas the Martyr's Day, 1931.

CONTENTS

LIST OF ILLUSTRATIONS

PLATES

IN THE TEXT

ST. THOMAS BECKET
IN ART

CHAPTER I

THE LIFE AND PERSONALITY OF ST. THOMAS BECKET

THERE are very few characters not only in the twelfth century but in the Middle Ages generally of which we can form as vivid an idea as of St. Thomas Becket. The information concerning him is abundant, and extraordinarily minute as well as demonstrably on the whole very reliable, even if somewhat contradictory on various points : and from it all, there emerges a picture of his personality which is singularly full of human interest. It was naturally the tragic climax of his life's story, which, retro-actively, made that story an object of so much attention on the part of numerous writers : but it is also quite obvious, that the whole of his career provided them, perfectly objectively, with material of exceptional attraction.

It is perhaps worth while here very briefly to re-capitulate the chief facts of Becket's life : in doing so, I shall necessarily traverse ground very familiar to many of my readers, but the practical utility of such a résumé will, I hope, be evident when the main argument of this volume is reached.

1

Thomas Becket did not live to a great age : for, as
the date of his birth is presumably 1118, he was only
about fifty-two when he met his death in 1170.   Of
Norman stock, and the son of Gilbert, probably a
merchant though of gentle birth, and his wife, Mahatz,
he was born in London ; and " Thomas of London "
was the designation of himself that he preferred all
through his life.   Merton in Surrey, London, and
possibly Paris denote successive stages in his early
education, in the course of which the claims of sport
and of knightly accomplishments on horseback were
not neglected : and a famous incident of his boyhood
is that of a mishap which he experienced one day
when out hawking with a friend of his father, Richer
de l'Aigle.   In crossing a mill stream by a narrow
plank, his horse slipped and both it and the rider
fell into the water, escaping, however, by what was
eventually regarded as a miracle, from being dragged
under the wheel of the mill.[1]   When young Becket was
free of his schools, it is notable that he did not by any
means immediately enter upon the career of an
ecclesiastic.   On the contrary, it is on record that—
cultivating, as we may assume, all the while a keen
interest in athletics and sport—he at first gained some
experience in business and civil administration ; until
about 1142 he became a member of the household
of Theobald, the learned Archbishop of Canterbury,
entering minor orders, and though he afterwards was
ordained deacon, it was as late as twenty years after
his first association with Theobald, when in 1162
he had been elected the latter's successor, that he
was ordained a priest.   He accompanied Theobald
when the latter in 1143 visited Rome, and subse-

---

[1] For an interesting synopsis of the different versions of this
story see Edwin A. Abbott, *St. Thomas of Canterbury, His Death and
Miracles*, London, 1898, Vol. I, p. 216 *seqq.*

quently for periods of considerable length devoted himself to the study of Canon law in such celebrated centres of learning as Bologna and Auxerre. Thus grounded, he was eventually able, in 1154, to take up the important office of archdeacon of Canterbury : but not for long. There now enters upon the scene the founder of the Plantagenet dynasty, Henry of Anjou, second of the name among the Kings of England and destined to remain henceforth in the closest contact with Becket, for good or for evil, as long as the latter lived. In 1155, when still on the right side of forty, Becket was appointed Chancellor of England, his sovereign, aged twenty-one, being very considerably his junior : and the accounts of the first friendly association of the two are not lacking in traits indicative of a boisterous, school-boyish mentality on either side. Vividness of speech, it may here be remarked, remained a characteristic of Becket all his life : he gave particularly striking proof of it in his exchange of words with his four assailants in Canterbury Cathedral.

As Chancellor, when conflicts with the Church occurred, Becket sponsored the cause of the King with great firmness : so much so, indeed, that even when Becket had joined the ranks of the martyred saints, this was not wholly forgotten : *Adolescens fere Saulus—Præsul factus vere Paulus—Commutavit studium* is the unequivocal reference to this phase of Becket's career in a hymn[1] known from a MS. written at Segovia in the fourteenth century. The achievements of Becket as head of the royal Chancery were great and of lasting importance : but the aspect of Becket the Chancellor which above all forces itself upon one's attention is that which shows him—another Julius II or Richelieu—as taking an active part in several of Henry II's campaigns : in Northern France in 1156, in Wales in 1157 and more

---

[1] G. M. Dreves, *Analecta Hymnica*, Vol. IX, No. 353.

particularly in Southern France and Normandy in 1159. Nor must reference be omitted to the unexampled splendour with which Becket surrounded his embassy to Louis VII, King of France, in 1158, when he went to Paris to negotiate—as he did successfully—the marriage between Henry, the eldest son of his sovereign (then a boy of three) and Margaret, daughter of the King of France.

When, in 1161, on the death of Theobald, the see of Canterbury fell vacant, Becket was Henry's selection for the succession. The Archbishop-designate was none too eager to fall in with this choice, and made it quite clear that in his new position he would have to take up an attitude very much at variance with that which had been his as Chancellor : but his objections were over-ruled, and on June 3, 1162, having first been ordained priest, he was solemnly enthroned as Archbishop of Canterbury.

In Becket's personal life, the ascetic tendency, which had certainly not been absent earlier in his life, not unnaturally became very much more pronounced after his elevation to the highest ecclesiastical office in England, though not so as completely to obliterate interests which until then had been very important to him : the evidence of his earliest biographers and of tradition is very strong on this point. As to his relations with Henry II, they were very soon affected by controversial questions which inevitably presented themselves. Not for nearly two years, however, did matters come to a head ; and the occasion when this happened was supplied by the council of bishops and barons summoned by Henry to meet in January 1164 at the Palace of Clarendon near Salisbury—a hunting lodge, which in the next century Henry III caused to be extensively enlarged and splendidly decorated with wall paintings, but of which now next to nothing remains. The question at issue was that concerning the jurisdiction over ecclesiastics : the King claiming far greater powers in this respect than he had hitherto been acknowledged to possess. Becket strongly opposed the King's designs. A discussion of the merits of the case would take us too far in the present connection : it must, however, be emphasized that it would be quite mistaken to attempt to decide the question on superficial and specious modern analogies ; and we may also recall the dictum of one of the profoundest students of Becket and his position in English history, the late Dr. W. H. Hutton, Dean of Winchester, to the effect that the mediæval church, " Slowly by her action in defence of her own claims . . . made natiònal liberty possible."[1]

At length Becket yielded and signified his assent to the " Constitutions of Clarendon " : soon afterwards, however, he again took up his former stand, refusing to seal the document embodying the Constitutions which had been drawn up. He was now in open conflict with his sovereign : and the latter, deeply incensed, summoned him to appear at a council held at Northampton a few months later, when he had to answer to various trumped-up charges, mainly relating to his accounts during the period when he had been Chancellor. Eventually the whole question of the Constitutions of Clarendon came up again ; and finding nothing but enmity against him in all quarters, Becket now decided upon a drastic step—he rode away in the night, crossing from Sandwich to the coast of Flanders on November 2, 1164. His goal was Sens, the beautiful cathedral city on the banks of the Yonne, where Pope Alexander III, himself an exile at the time, was then residing : and on his way there, Becket was received with great honour at Soissons by Louis VII, whom, as

[1] W. H. Hutton, *Thomas Becket*, second edition, Cambridge, 1926, p. 274.

we saw, he had originally known under very different
conditions. Finally, he got to Sens, where he set out
his cause to the Pope, with the result that the vast
majority of the Constitutions of Clarendon were re-
jected. He did not, however, linger long in Sens,
but proceeded at the end of November to the
great Cistercian abbey of Pontigny, lying secluded
among the woods some thirty miles beyond Sens :
and at Pontigny he remained for the next two
years.

Meanwhile, neither Henry II nor Becket's many
other enemies had been idle : he was denounced, without however any result, to Louis VII and the Pope,
and as a particularly savage reprisal the whole of
Becket's kindred was exiled from England. From his
refuge at Pontigny, Becket continued to remonstrate
vehemently, and eventually, on Whit Sunday 1166 at
Vézelay, pronounced sentence of excommunication
against several of his enemies—among whom, however, Henry II was not included. Threats of reprisal
by the latter against the Cistercian order in England
forced Becket to leave his asylum at Pontigny in November 1166 : he now settled in Sens, and the next few
years were taken up by a seemingly interminable series
of attempts to remedy the situation, Becket displaying
a tenacity which at times to some extent alienated from
him many sympathies—even those of King Louis, for
instance. When, in January 1169, the sovereigns of
England and France met at Montmirail (in Maine,
within Henry II's French dominions) Becket repaired
there also, but no satisfactory result ensued from the
stormy interview between him and his king or from a
further meeting between the two in Paris in November
the same year. The action of Henry in causing his
eldest son, Henry, to be crowned by the Archbishop of
York, assisted by the Bishops of London and Salisbury,

in Westminster Abbey on June 14, 1170, still further complicated the situation : for this was done in contravention of an order of the Pope, which laid down that the privilege of performing the act of coronation pertained to the exiled Archbishop of Canterbury. This brought the King of England within imminent danger of excommunication : and events now moved rapidly towards a reconciliation with Becket, which took place little more than a month later, at Fréteval in Normandy, on July 20, 1170.

Of this reconciliation Becket has given a graphic account in a long letter to the Pope : and it is evident that on that occasion a genuine goodwill was displayed by the two antagonists who had once been such close friends and that the close of the era of hostility was a source of great happiness to both. They met twice again —at Tours and at Chaumont—but meanwhile various things had occurred to endanger the harmony just restored ; and when, on December 1, Becket crossed over from Wissant to Sandwich, he had sown the seed of the final and fatal conflict by suspending the Archbishop of York and renewing the sentence of excommunication previously passed on the Bishops of London and Salisbury. However, his journey from Sandwich to Canterbury was one triumphal progress, and December 2, when he re-entered Canterbury after an absence of over six years, was afterwards kept as a church feast, that of the *Regressio Sancti Thomæ*.[1] There arose also quickly a tendency to establish a parallel between the last days of St. Thomas and the Passion of Christ : and we may here recall the words of the Early South English Legen-

---

[1] My friend Mr. Francis Wormald has identified in a burnt fragment of a fourteenth-century Breviary in the Library of the Dean and Chapter at Canterbury a small portion of the office for the feast of the *Regressio* and intends publishing his find in the *Analecta Bollandiana*.

dary with reference to Becket's progress to Canterbury, which occurred, be it remembered, at Advent-time :

> Ase ore louerd a-palme-sonenday : honovred was i-nov₃
> þo he rod into Jerusalem : and toward is deþe drov₃
> Al-so was þis holi man : ase men mi₃ten i-seo þere
> For ore louerd wolde þat is deth : semblable to his were.[1]

Clamorous though his welcome was, there was yet evidence of enmity as well. When a week after his return, Becket attempted to see the young King Henry at Woodstock he met with a rebuff, although he had characteristically tried to conciliate his former pupil by a gift of three magnificent horses[2] and Ranulf de Broc, who by the King's authority had installed himself in the archiepiscopal castle of Saltwood, and who was one of the people excommunicated at Vézelay, went out of his way to be vexatious and insulting.

Meanwhile, the three bishops, against whom Thomas, by direction of the Pope, had taken such stern action, had repaired to lay their complaints before the King in Normandy, at the Castle of Bur near Bayeux : and at the conclusion of the interview Henry in a fit of temper

---

[1] A translation of this into modern English is as follows :

As Our Lord on Palm Sunday : honoured was enough
Though he rode into Jerusalem : and towards his death drove
So was this holy man : so that men might see there
For Our Lord would that his death : similar to his were.

(See " The Early South English Legendary," ed. Horstmann, *Early English Text Society*, 1887 ; p. 159 *seq.*, v. 1855–58.)

Earlier suggestions of the same parallel occur, for instance, in Herbert of Bosham (*Materials for the History of Thomas Becket*, ed. J. C. Robertson, Vol. III, p. 478) and John of Salisbury (*ibid.*, Vol. II, p. 318).

[2] It may be mentioned, incidentally, that the coronation of Henry, the cause of so much trouble, was to no purpose : he died before his father, in 1183, and the successor of Henry II was, of course, his younger son Richard Cœur-de-Lion, born at Oxford in 1157.

let fall the famous words : " What sluggard wretches, what cowards have I brought up in my court who care nothing for their allegiance to their master : not one will deliver me from this low-born priest ! " On this, four knights among the courtiers—Reginald Fitzurse, Hugh de Moreville, William de Tracy and Richard le Bret or Breton—decided upon immediate action. Crossing the Channel, they forgathered at Saltwood Castle on December 28, and on the next day proceeded to Canterbury. An interview with Becket at the archiepiscopal palace found him unyielding on the question of the three bishops : and after the knights had withdrawn and Becket proceeded to the Cathedral, there then followed the tragedy in the part of the transept known ever since as " The Martyrdom."[1]

It is difficult to give an adequate idea of the horror with which the news of the murder of Becket was received throughout the Christian world. In expiation of the deed, suggested by a hasty saying of his, Henry II not only had to yield over the disputed points of the Constitutions of Clarendon,[2] but also to submit to a lengthy programme of penance, culminating in the solemn act at Canterbury in July 1174. The year before, the martyred Archbishop had been canonized. His cult now spread all over Europe with lightning speed and the consequences of this were very soon to be seen in all the arts : indeed, the Middle Ages supply no quite comparable case before his time, and after him the nearest analogy is only afforded in the next century by St. Francis of Assisi, whose international effect upon the arts was, however, of much slower growth—on the

[1] Of the details of this episode, an account is given further on (p. 70 *seqq.*).

[2] On this question see the illuminating article by Mr. Z. N. Brooke, " The Effect of Becket's Murder on Papal Authority in England," in *The Cambridge Historical Journal*, Vol. II, No. 3, 1928, pp. 213–228.

other hand St. Thomas never had the good fortune to inspire a Giotto. It is evident that the diffusion of the veneration of St. Thomas was much helped by the fact that Henry II's three daughters all married in different countries, Joan indeed twice, first in Sicily and then in the South of France, Mathilda in Germany and Eleanor in Spain. Canterbury now also quickly rose to the position of one of the principal centres of pilgrimage in Europe ; and in addition to the Day of St. Thomas which fell in midwinter—on December 29—the anniversary of the translation of his bones to a magnificent shrine on July 7, 1220—in the first " Jubilee " year of the saint's death—became the second great occasion in the year devoted to the veneration of the saint, and indeed outstripping the first in importance since it occurred at a season when pilgrims could move about with greater ease.[1] Six other great jubilees marked the veneration of St. Thomas Becket during the Middle Ages—1270, 1320, 1370, 1420, 1470 and 1520—the last jubilee occurring but eighteen years before the destruction of the shrine at the order of the very king who, together with the Emperor Charles V, in 1520 had himself worshipped before it, before proceeding to the Field of the Cloth of Gold.

From whatever angle we approach it, the cult of St. Thomas Becket provides a subject of the most absorbing interest to the student of mediæval civilization. The present volume is, however, primarily devoted to one particular aspect of this subject—the iconography of St. Thomas Becket. Much of the artistic production of different countries and centuries relating to the personality and life of St. Thomas has, of course, perished. In

---

[1] The offices of both days may be read in Procter and Wordsworth's edition of the Sarum Breviary (Cambridge, 1882) ; that of December 29 is particularly interesting in relation to the iconography of St. Thomas Becket.

England, after the de-canonization of " bysshop Becket," decreed by Henry VIII—as part of a campaign against the good name and fame of St. Thomas, most of the details of which do not immediately concern this enquiry —a veritable war was, in 1538, declared on the innumerable representations of the saint then existing in this country, the proclamation enacting expressly that " his ymages and pictures, through the hole realme, shall be putte downe and auoyded out of all churches, chapelles, and other places."[1] Where the destruction in obedience to this order was not complete, defacement of varying extent was resorted to, as is clear, for instance, from the many illuminations of manuscripts in which the renderings of St. Thomas Becket have been disfigured or partly obliterated.[2] Outside England, the toll of destruction, from various causes, has also been great : but, even so, there still exists plenty of documentation in England and elsewhere on which to base a study of the iconography of St. Thomas Becket : though we shall do well to remember that it is only a fraction of what originally existed.

[1] The whole of the passage relating to St. Thomas Becket in the proclamation issued from Westminster, on November 16, 1538, and dealing in its earlier part with heretical books, is printed in Appendix I, *postea*, page 109 *seq.* The argument directed against Becket is a most ingenious piece of special pleading.

[2] At Ashford in Kent, a curious attempt at compromise was made, inasmuch as the effigy of St. Thomas Becket, by removing the archiepiscopal cross and substituting for it a wool-comb, was transformed into one of St. Blaise. This compromise was, however, not allowed to pass muster. (See J. Gairdner, *Lollardy and the Reformation*, ii, 341.) The attempts at restoring the cult of St. Thomas during the reign of Mary Tudor and the iconoclastic excesses to which they led are vividly illuminated by the documents, printed in Appendix II, *postea*, p. 111.

CHAPTER II

SINGLE REPRESENTATIONS OF ST. THOMAS BECKET

IN attempting a survey of the iconography of St. Thomas Becket, the question must first be considered whether there exist any representations of the Archbishop dating from his lifetime.

The only category of examples that deserves serious attention in this connection is that formed by such seals as are either definitely known to have been used by the Archbishop himself or else are reputed to have been so used. Their number is not large—four in all ; and the one which is undeniably authentic[1]—a counterseal appended to a charter in the Public Record Office—is unfortunately quite irrelevant to our enquiry, as the figured portion of it is simply a classical intaglio of the god Mercury.[2] The three others all contain a conventional figure of an archbishop, in pontificals, with mitre and crozier, imparting the benediction. One of these seals must, however, undoubtedly be regarded as a forgery ; and another is probably nothing but a replica of the seal of St. Thomas's predecessor Theobald, with the inscription slightly recut—perhaps by a forger—so as to tally with the name of his successor. Of both the seals casts exist in the collection of the Society of Antiquaries. Of a

---

[1] Reproduced in *The Archæological Journal*, Vol. XXVI (1869), plate facing page 84. The inscription on the seal is : SIGILLVM TOME LVND+.

[2] One wonders if this was the " green gem " in the ring worn by St. Thomas at the time of his death, which subsequently came into the possession of the Abbey of Glastonbury.

third, only a woodcut is known, first published in the *Gentleman's Magazine* for 1848[1] : it has frequently been reproduced[2] and doubts on its authenticity were expressed as far back as 1869 by Mr. Albert Way.[3] I am told that some years ago it was recognized by the late Mr. Ready, cast-maker of the British Museum, as one of his father's imitations of mediæval seals,[4] and it rather adds to the piquancy of the situation that it was this Mr. Ready *père* who concurred in Mr. Way's doubts as to the genuineness of the two other examples.

The very earliest posthumous representation of St. Thomas Becket known to us is a single figure : it is the one which occurs among the Byzantine mosaics of the cathedral at Monreale in Sicily (Plate II, fig. 1) and as the whole building, mosaics and all, is understood to have been completed in an almost inexplicably brief period, between 1174 and 1182, this mosaic would at most be separated by twelve years from the date of the martyrdom. As to the reason which prompted the inclusion of this recently canonized saint among those represented in these mosaics who were of so much more ancient standing in the Catalogue of Saints, it is really not far to seek : for the builder of Monreale Cathedral, William the Good of Sicily, was in 1177 married to Princess Joan, daughter of Henry II of England. Whether, all circumstances considered, it could be regarded as " a compliment to his English bride," as it has been called, is another matter. The rendering of St. Thomas is a

---

[1] Cf. *The Gentleman's Magazine*, November 1848, Vol. XXX, N.S., p. 494.

[2] E.g. in J. R. Green, *A Short History of the English People*, illustrated edition, London, 1892, Vol. I, p. 201 ; and in Mr. Egerton Beck's article " The Mitre and Tiara in Heraldry and Ornament " in *The Burlington Magazine*, Vol. XXIII (August 1913), p. 263.

[3] See Albert Way in *Archæological Journal*, Vol. XXVI (1869), pp. 84-9.

[4] For this information I am indebted to Mr. Egerton Beck.

very simple one : he is shown in his mass vestments, with the pallium (the white band, ornamented
with black crosses, which is a vestment specially per-
taining to archbishops, and which usually is displayed
hanging down from his neck so as to form the outline
of a Y), without any indication of a mitre, holding a
book in his left hand and imparting the benediction
with his right. Of any emblem of his martyrdom there
is no trace ; and it would be impossible to expect from
this naturally very stylized figure a portrait-like character, such as, for instance, to some extent does attach
to the earliest thirteenth-century pictures of St. Francis
of Assisi. As to St. Thomas Becket's exterior, a passage
in one of the Icelandic *Thomas Sagas*, thought to reflect
the evidence of a person who had seen the Archbishop,
refers to him as " slim of growth and pale of hue, dark
of hair, with a long nose and straightly featured face."[1]

Closely similar to the Monreale figure is one, of but
slightly later date, which once was to be seen among
the wall paintings decorating the apse of the Oratory
of St. Sylvester in the ancient church of St. Martin and
St. Sylvester (San Martino ai Monti) on the Esquilin in
Rome. All these frescoes are lost, but tolerably accurate
seventeenth-century copies of them exist in a codex in

---

[1] Dean Stanley (*Memorials of Canterbury*, 7th ed., 1875, p. 196)
has pointed out that the tall stature of St. Thomas, explicitly
mentioned by William Fitzstephen, is borne witness to by the
length of the vestments of St. Thomas preserved in the treasury of
Sens Cathedral. " On the feast of ' St. Thomas ' till very recently,
they were worn for that one day by the officiating priest. The
tallest priest was always selected—and, even then, it was necessary
to pin them up." A note (fifteenth century) in the Lambeth MS.
306, fol. 203, on " The longitude of men folowyng," beginning with
" Moyses, xiijfote & viij ynches & di " mentions as seventh in the
list of eight notable people " Seynt Thomas of Caunterbery, vij
fote save a ynche " (" Three Fifteenth-Century Chronicles," ed.
James Gairdner, *Camden Society*, New Series, Vol. XXVIII, 1880,
p. 27).

PLATE II

1. MOSAIC, MONREALE
LATE TWELFTH CENTURY

2. FRESCO (DESTROYED), ROME,
SAN MARTINO AI MONTI
EARLY THIRTEENTH CENTURY

3. WALL-PAINTING, HAUXTON CHURCH
THIRTEENTH CENTURY

PLATE III

3. FRESCO, SACRO SPECO, SUBIACO
c. 1260

4. STAINED GLASS FRAGMENT, FAIRFORD
FOURTEENTH CENTURY

1. STATUE ON THE FRONT OF
WELLS CATHEDRAL
THIRTEENTH CENTURY

2. SILVER MEDALLION,
BRITISH MUSEUM
SEVENTEENTH CENTURY

5. (A) ANONYMOUS
ETCHING
SEVENTEENTH CENTURY

(B) ETCHING BY
W. HOLLAR
BRITISH MUSEUM

the Vatican Library (*Cod. Barb. lat.* 4405). The figure
which interests us (Plate II, fig. 2) occurred in a row
of four full-lengths of saints, painted underneath the
semi-dome of the apse : St. Agnes, St. Eusebius of
Vercelli, St. Thomas Becket and St. Cecilia.[1] The
person who caused these frescoes to be painted was
Cardinal Uguccione ; and their date is the very begin-
nings of the thirteenth century.

Of renderings of St. Thomas of the simplest type,
exemplified at Monreale and San Martino ai Monti and
showing him as the archbishop, *tout court*, without any
further emblems, there exists an enormous number ; it is,
of course, iconographically much the least interesting
category, though many of the examples which it com-
prises are far from unimportant artistically. Among wall
paintings a notable early instance is seen in a fresco of
about 1260, in the Sacro Speco at Subiaco (Plate III, fig. 3)
in which St. Thomas, decidedly youthful in appearance
and in vestments which include the pallium, is depicted
seated between St. Stephen and St. Nicholas. Presumably of not much later date are the two figures of
bishops, painted on the wall of the Campanile of the
Priory of St. Thomas of Canterbury lying between Arco
and Riva on the Lago di Garda and founded in 1194 :
one of them is doubtless to be interpreted as the patron
Saint of the Priory. Still keeping to Italy, but advancing far across the centuries, we note the presence of
St. Thomas as a half-length profile, holding the martyr's
palm and with his mitre inscribed " S. Thoma,"
lost among the myriads of saints occurring on the
predella, now in the National Gallery, of Fra Angelico's
altarpiece for San Domenico at Fiesole (1420–25).
In this instance the Saint has no pallium ; and the

---

[1] See the reproduction of the entire copy in the Barberini codex
given by J. Wilpert, *Die römischen Mosaiken und Malereien der
Kirchlichen Bauten*, Vol. I (Freiburg, i. B., 1917), p. 336, Fig. 110.

same remark applies to the majority of the representations of St. Thomas Becket in all countries. The pallium is thus also missing—to continue with Italian examples—in the picture of 1504, by Timoteo Viti, in the sacristy of the Duomo of Urbino (Plate IV), in which St. Thomas is seen seated on the left as a youthful, mitred bishop holding a long cross with a crystal shaft ; while in 1520 we find him enthroned old and bearded, mitred, but again pallium-less, as the principal figure of a picture of very Bellinesque character by Girolamo da Santa Croce in the church of San Silvestro at Venice (Plate V). It is interesting to note in this connection that at Venice St. Thomas was venerated as the patron of the wine coopers[1] ; just as in London he was the patron saint of the Company of Brewers.[2] As to the reasons for this we may note for

[1] See G. Ludwig in *Jahrbuch der königlich preussischen Kunstsammlungen*, Vol. XXIX, 1903, supplement, p. 18. The earliest representation of St. Thomas in Venice known to me occurs at the back of the great altarpiece of 1443 by Antonio Vivarini and Giovanni d'Alemagna, above the high altar of the Cappella di San Tarasio in the church of San Zaccaria.

[2] I am indebted to Mr. A. W. Clapham, F.S.A., for pointing this out to me. In this connection it may be noted that the Worshipful Company of Brewers possesses an embroidered pall of the early sixteenth century, containing as part of its scheme of decoration two half-length figures of St. Thomas Becket and the arms attributed to the Archbishop, impaled with those of the Company. The coat of arms posthumously assigned to St. Thomas displays the arms of the Archbishop of Canterbury impaling three *beckets* or choughs —a canting device based on the Norman French word *becquet* which, in the sense of "small bird" is still, I understand, used in Guernsey. The earliest rendering of these arms on a monumental scale, known to me, occurs in the series of arms in the Cathedral Cloisters at Canterbury, the work on which was taken in hand by Prior Chillenden 1391–1411 : see R. Griffin, in *Archæologia*, Vol. LXVI (1915), Plate XXXIV, fig. 2.

I will not attempt to make a census of the various examples of these arms existing in different places, but limit myself to noting that one rendering occurs in the seventeenth-century glass in the Court Room of the Brewers Hall, Cricklegate, while another may

one thing that there are quite a number of facts in the life of Becket which associate him somewhat pointedly with the partaking of wine. Such is the circumstance reported by William FitzStephen, that although his general drink was water in which hay had been boiled, he always would insist on taking the first taste of the wine and then gave it to those who were at table with him. Also, there is the story that before he went to meet his fate he had drunk more wine than usual, and when this was pointed out to him he replied, " He who must lose much blood, must needs drink much wine." And one or two further incidents pointing in the same direction might be quoted, as also his reputed power of changing water into wine, said to have been exercised on one occasion in the presence of the Pope.[1] Then, as to beer : FitzStephen refers particularly to the two vehicles, containing beer in iron-bound casks, which were a *pièce de resistance* of St. Thomas's impressive ambassadorial progress to Paris in 1158. There is further the miracle, related by Master Richard, monk of Ely, which occurred when two poor people, Ralph of Hadfield and his wife, wanted to go on a pilgrimage to Canterbury, but were without the necessary funds. They thought they would raise some by making some beer and selling it : but the beer would not ferment. The woman then lowered into it a phial containing some of St. Thomas's blood : and a most successful fermentation followed.[2]

be seen among the arms carved on a late fifteenth-century altar tomb in West Ham Church, accompanying the effigy of a man who, to judge by other coats of arms on this tomb, had a connection with the brewing trade. The chapel of St. Thomas Becket in East Dereham Church, Norfolk, is mentioned by Dr. Montague James (*Suffolk and Norfolk*, London, 1930, p. 184) as having an old painted ceiling " diapered with crowns and T's."

[1] See Edwin A. Abbott, *St. Thomas of Canterbury, his Death and Miracles*, London, 1898, Vol. II, p. 7 *seq.*

[2] Edwin A. Abbott, *op. cit.*, Vol. I, p. 328.

Of English mediæval wall paintings of St. Thomas as
the archbishop, that in Hauxton Church, Cambridge-
shire, dating from the thirteenth century (Plate II, fig. 3)
may be singled out for special mention both on account
of its high artistic quality and because of its excellent
state of preservation.   In this instance, the figure wears
a pallium ; and the simple hieratic attitude—the right
hand raised in the act of blessing, the left hand holding
the cross-staff—was to become a very frequent one in
English representations of St. Thomas in different
mediums.   It probably recurred in the fine, but greatly
injured figure which has its place in a group of three
martyrs, between St. Edmund and St. Stephen, on a
division of the vaulting of the Relic Chamber of Norwich Cathedral, the paintings in question dating from
the end of the thirteenth century.[1]   Originally no doubt
also a notable work, but now unfortunately very much
faded, is the large cognate figure of St. Thomas on the
southern face of one of the four western Norman piers
in St. Albans Cathedral, dating from the late fourteenth
century.[2]

Finally, within the domain of English mediæval painting, we may note that representations of St. Thomas as

---

[1] For a reproduction see Tancred Borenius and E. W. Tristram,
English Mediæval Painting, Florence, 1926, Plate XXXVI.

[2] A water-colour copy of this painting by M. F. Gray is in the
Victoria and Albert Museum.   Other examples of the type now
under discussion in English mediæval wall-painting occur at
Ampney Crucis, Glos., North Transept, *c.* 1300 (copy by Prof.
E. W. Tristram, Victoria and Albert Museum) ; Fairford, Glos. (with
a representation of the Canterbury shrine) ; Hadleigh, Essex, *c.* 1200
(inscribed " Beate Tomas " ; *Royal Commission on Historical Monuments, Essex*, Vol. IV, p. 63) ; Lower Halston Church, Kent (see
Archæologia Cantiana, Vol. XXXIII, pp. 157, 163 *seq.*, with a
reproduction) ; Maidstone, Kent (All Saints' Church) ; Merstham,
Surrey (very faint) ; Shorthampton, Oxon (see P. M. Johnston
in *Archæological Journal*, Vol. LXII, 1905, pp. 164 *seq.*, with
reproduction, date *c.* 1460, with simple straight pallium, the face
beardless) ; Wellow, Hants.

PLATE IV

PAINTING BY TIMOTEO VITI, DUOMO, URBINO
1504

PLATE V

PAINTING BY GIROLAMO DA SANTA CROCE,
SAN SILVESTRO, VENICE
1520

archbishop without any additional attributes occur fairly frequently among the surviving panel pictures of the late fifteenth and early sixteenth centuries painted for the decoration of the roodscreens of the churches, notably in East Anglia and Devonshire.[1] Artistically, these pictures are, however, but seldom of any consequence.

Of examples from German mediæval painting illustrating the type now under discussion, I may mention that which occurs in a composition of the Crucifixion in the chapel of the Bülow family in the church of Doberan in Mecklenburg[2] : unfortunately in recent times this painting has been so heavily " restored " as to possess next to no value as a document. It is, however, of interest as the first illustration, to which I have occasion to refer, of the very considerable diffusion of the cult of the English saint in Germany : and as we shall see, the iconography of St. Thomas Becket derives material from many different regions of Germany, although a number of particularly important examples are localised in that coastal district of the North Sea and the Baltic to which Doberan belongs. No doubt trade connections with England were in those parts largely responsible for the popularity of the cult of St. Thomas.

Turning now to representations other than paintings of St. Thomas as merely the archbishop, we may at first call attention to a few examples of sculpture of more

[1] E.g. at Attleborough, Binham Abbey, Burlingham St. Andrew's (dated 1530), Horsham St. Faith (on pulpit, dated 1480), Oxburgh, Ranworth, Sparham, Stalham, Worstead, all in Norfolk ; at Nayland and Somerleyton, in Suffolk ; at Ashton, Hoxne, Plymtree and Woolborough, in Devonshire ; at West Clandon, Surrey (reproduced in *Surrey Archæological Collections*, Vol. XXI, 1908, plate facing p. 99) ; and at Strensham, Worcestershire.

[2] *Die Kunst-und Geschichtsdenkmäler des Grossherzogthums Mecklenburg-Schwerin*, III, 660. For a photograph of this painting and of an old tracing of the composition, I am indebted to Prof. R. Sedlmaier of Rostock University.

than average interest.[1]   One is the noble late twelfth-
century statue, or rather high relief, which has been let
into the wall of the ambulatory of Sens Cathedral, and
which comes from the house traditionally said to have
been inhabited by St. Thomas during his stay at Sens
(Plate VI, fig. 1). Another, of much later date, is a very
striking presentment, in carved wood, of the enthroned
archbishop, formerly in the church of Skepptuna in
the province of Uppland, Sweden, and now in the
Historical Museum at Stockholm (Plate VI, fig. 2).[2] The
inscription on the halo discloses the identity of the saint,
and the whole is a fine example of late Gothic realism,
of about 1475, not improbably by the same artist,
Bernt Notke of Lübeck, as the celebrated group of
St. George and the Dragon in the Storkyrka in Stockholm.   Yet another example from Scandinavia occurs
in one of the four figures of saints, in carved wood
(St. Thomas Becket, St. Olaf, St. Edmund and St.
Magnus Dux, the local saint of the Orkney Islands), of
an altarpiece dating from the fifteenth century, formerly
in the church of Lurø in Northern Norway and now in
Bergen Museum (Plate VI, fig. 3).

As we shall see, a very remarkable rendering of the
Martyrdom of St. Thomas exists on a reliquary in
Norway ;[3] and altogether, in view of the close artistic

---

[1] Mr. Eric Maclagan has kindly drawn my attention to the
fact that on the keystone of one of the arches of the south doorway
of the church of Barfreston, Kent (reproduced in E. S. Prior and
A. Gardner, *An Account of Medieval Figure Sculpture in England*,
Cambridge, 1912, Fig. 175), there occurs a half-length figure of a
bishop which has often been interpreted as representing St. Thomas
Becket. As the doorway has been dated as early as about 1170,
this identification, if correct, would of course be extremely interesting ; but it is scarcely possible to establish it, and it strikes me that
the balance of probability is in favour of the figure being of a more
generically emblematic character.

[2] A copy of this statue was in 1930 presented to Canterbury
Cathedral.

[3] See *postea*, p. 76.

and other relations existing between Norway and England in the Middle Ages, we are justified in assuming that St. Thomas Becket was frequently represented in Norway during that period. It is a matter of history that Eystein, third Archbishop of Norway (1161-88), during his three years of exile in Southern England, was greatly struck by the building activities at Canterbury, where St. Thomas had then been but recently slain : and Trondhjem Cathedral bears to this day the impress of many ideas derived from Canterbury. It is hence difficult to imagine St. Thomas's effigy as not having been included among those which formed such an imposing array of saints on the west front of Trondhjem Cathedral (thirteenth century), among the surviving examples being a St. Denys (or St. Nicaise) and a headless, indeterminate ecclesiastic.[1] Again, an early Gothic figure of a bishop, from Granvin Church, now in Bergen Museum,[2] though anonymous, shows the typical " St. Thomas Becket attitude " which we have seen exemplified in the Hauxton painting.

Of extant English examples of sculpture in stone, one of the earliest is probably the one, dating from the fourteenth century, which occurs among the figures carved on the jambs of the doorways of the Chapter House at Haughmond Abbey, Shropshire. It shows St. Thomas Becket with a crossstaff next to St. Augustine as an abbot with a crozier.[3]

In the eastern apsidal chapel of Henry VII's chapel in Westminster Abbey a figure of St. Nicholas of Bari and one of an archbishop, with cross-staff reading a book, now flank an empty pedestal, which bears the initials

[1] Reproduced in Harry Fett, *Billedhuggerkunsten i Norge under Sverreaetten* (Christiania, 1908), Figs. 124, 125.

[2] Harry Fett, *op. cit.*, Fig. 109.

[3] See W. H. St. John Hope, in *The Archæological Journal*, Vol. LXVI (1909), p. 296.

H.R. (Plate I). This has been interpreted as showing
that Henry VII intended to place in the niche a statue
of Henry VI, as soon as the latter had been declared a
saint ; and colour is undoubtedly lent to this surmise
by the proximity of the figure of St. Nicholas, for whom
Henry VI had a particular devotion. The figure on
the right is usually identified with St. Thomas Becket,[1]
and such an interpretation is indeed very possible seeing
that when the chapel was built an effigy of him is sure
to have been included in the general scheme of decoration. On the other hand there is nothing very definitely
indicating the archbishop as being St. Thomas Becket ;
there is one empty niche, in the southern apsidal chapel,
between effigies of St. Denys and St. Paul, where an
effigy of St. Thomas might have stood ; and it is a little
difficult to imagine that a figure of St. Thomas Becket
would have been allowed to survive in so prominent
and exposed a position. Of the smaller statues in niches
in the triforium of Henry VII's chapel, one of an archbishop on the north side has also been thought possibly
to represent St. Thomas Becket,[2] but certainty on this
point is scarcely attainable.[3]

It would indeed have been satisfactory if at any rate
one indubitable statue of St. Thomas Becket dating
from the Middle Ages had remained intact in London :
for the veneration in which St. Thomas was held in his
native city during that period was very great—a vast subject this which here can only be hinted at—and his effigy
met one then in London in many contexts. The chapel

---

[1] Compare *Westminster Abbey* (*Royal Commission on Historical
Monuments*), London, 1924, p. 63 and Plate 204.

[2] *Ibid.*, p. 65, No. 92 and Plate 213.

[3] The chapel of SS. Edmund and Thomas the Martyr, one of
the ambulatory chapels at Westminster Abbey, is now bereft of any
material bearing on the iconography of St. Thomas Becket. Concerning an altar frontal formerly at Westminster Abbey and
embroidered with a representation of the Martyrdom, see *postea*,
p. 83, n. 5.

PLATE VI

1. HIGH RELIEF, SENS
CATHEDRAL

LATE TWELFTH CENTURY

2. STATUE IN CARVED WOOD,
HISTORICAL MUSEUM,
STOCKHOLM

NORTH GERMAN, C. 1475

3. STATUE, CARVED
WOOD, BERGEN
MUSEUM

NORTH GERMAN
FIFTEENTH CENTURY

4. STONE EFFIGY,
ARBROATH ABBEY

FIFTEENTH CENTURY

5. STATUE, TORO CATHEDRAL

STYLE OF BERRUGUETE, C. 1540–50

6. RELIEF, SILVER
TRIPTYCH

AUGSBURG, 1492

PLATE VII

PAINTING BY FELICE BRUSASORZI, SAN TOMMASO
CANTUARIENSE, VERONA
1579

which stood on old London Bridge was dedicated to St. Thomas. It formed part—as an edifice in the Early English style—of the structure begun in the reign of Henry II by Peter of Colechurch and completed in 1209 ; and it was entirely rebuilt, in perpendicular Gothic, between 1384 and 1396. One wonders what material it can have contained for the iconography of St. Thomas. The evidence of the records is suggestive and tantalizing : in 1539–40, a painter of Southwark was paid 2s. for the " defasynge and mendynge of divers pyctures of Thomas Beckett in Our Lady Chapell," the dedication of the chapel having meanwhile been changed in obedience to Henry VIII's order. Similarly, we find an embroiderer as late as 1543 showing really remarkable skill in transforming, on some piece of needlework belonging to the chapel, a Martyrdom of St. Thomas into " the image of Our Lady." An indenture of 24 Edward III—thus *c.* 1351—mentions among the objects in the chapel " 2 linen cloths for covering the cross and the image of St. Thomas of Canterbury before the altar."[1] Moreover, we know that the seal of the chapel, dating from the end of the thirteenth century, showed the figure of the archbishop, seated, imparting the benediction, above a representation of the bridge, under the arch of which the prow of a boat was seen on the water : the inscription on the seal, as far as ascertainable, ran

SIGILL' BEATI THOM . . . RTIRIS D' PONTE LON. . . .[2]

Up to 1539, the Common Seal of the Corporation of London, designed in the thirteenth century, also contained a figure of St. Thomas, seated between groups of worshippers, laymen on the left and clergymen on the right, while a prospect of the City of London

[1] See Gordon Home, *Old London Bridge*, London, 1931, pp. 167, 102.

[2] See W. de G. Birch, *Catalogue of Seals in the Department of MSS. in the British Museum*, Vol. I (1887), Nos. 3561, 3562.

appeared under a semicircular arch below the feet of
St. Thomas, and an inscription touchingly invoked the
protection of St. Thomas on his native city :

ME QUAE TE PEPERI NE CESSES THOMA TUERI.

In 1539, but not until fairly late in the year, September 28, this seal was replaced by the City Arms.[1]   The
Hospital " of St. Thomas of Acon " in London also had
a thirteenth- to fourteenth-century seal, containing a
representation of St. Thomas enthroned.[2]   Again, in the
now empty niche on the Water or Lollards' Tower of
Lambeth Palace there once stood facing the river a
figure of the martyred Archbishop " to which the water-
men of the Thames doffed their caps as they rowed by
in their countless barges."[3]

In this connection a word must be added about representations of St. Thomas as archbishop in two provinces
of English mediæval sculpture—that formed by the
ivories and that comprising the alabaster " tables " and
figures.   The number of ivories here to be noticed is
very small : there is one indubitable example occurring
on the sinister wing of a triptych in the British Museum,
which heraldic evidence indicates as having been made
for John Grandisson, Bishop of Exeter, between 1327
and 1369[4] : and here the presence of the Archbishop
(who is shown wearing the pallium) is doubtless ac-
counted for by the special veneration for St. Thomas
entertained by Bishop Grandisson who is the author of
a Life of the saint.   The attitude of the figure is here
roughly that of the Hauxton painting : the right hand

    [1] For a reproduction of the thirteenth-century seal see *Proceed-
ings of the Society of Antiquaries*, second series, Vol. XV (1893–95),
p. 443.   W. de G. Birch, *op. cit.*, No. 5068.
    [2] W. de G. Birch, *op. cit.*, No. 3557.
    [3] A. P. Stanley, *op. cit.*, p. 199.
    [4] Reproduced in M. H. Longhurst, *English Ivories*, London,
1926, Pl. 45.

raised in benediction, the cross-staff held in the left hand
—a pose which, if there is no definite indication to the
contrary, in English mediæval art may be said to create
a strong presumption in favour of the figure being St.
Thomas Becket. Another ivory which also was made for
John Grandisson and was acquired for the British
Museum in 1926,[1] shows a figure of a bishop in the
same place as the ivory first mentioned, and he is
most probably also to be identified with St. Thomas,
although he has no pallium and the pose is different—
he holds the cross-staff in his right hand and a book
in his left.

The conventional " St. Thomas Becket attitude " just
referred to is seen in one of the alabaster figures which
occur on one of the magnificent mediæval tombs in
Harewood Church. It is the altar tomb conjecturally
assigned to Richard Redmayne (*ob.* 1476/77) and his
wife and adorned with an artistically as well as iconographically most interesting series of figures of saints.[2]
Among single English alabaster " tables " or figures one
comes across numerous effigies of bishops, several of
which doubtless are intended for St. Thomas Becket,
though it is difficult to speak with certainty in most
cases. There is, however, no doubt that the figure of
an archbishop with cross-staff and book (or in the act
of blessing) which invariably occurs on the conventional
" St. John's Heads " as a pendant to the figure of
St. Peter, is intended for St. Thomas Becket.[3] There

---

[1] Reproduced *ibid.* supplementary plate (p. 171).

[2] Next to this figure (the second from the left on the south side)
is one of a bishop holding the upper part of his head in his right
hand. Though the figure has some resemblance to a type of
St. Thomas Becket representation which can be paralleled in
England (see below, p. 36) it is, however, probably intended for
another saint.

[3] See W. H. St. John Hope in *Archæologia*, Vol. LII (1890),
pp. 669–708. Examples may be seen in the Victoria and Albert
Museum, the collection of Dr. W. L. Hildburgh, the British Museum,

has been a tendency of late years to identify the figure
with St. William of York ; but not only was St. Thomas
Becket a much more widely known saint—there exists a
passage in a will of 1522 in which reference is made to
" a Seynt Johis hede of alabast' wt Seynt Pet' and
Seynt Thomas."[1]   In addition, it may be noted, that
St. Peter's day occurring on June 29, and St. Thomas
Becket's exactly half a year later, on December 29, here
was a juxtaposition which must have greatly appealed
to the mediæval mind.[2]

In Scotland, the great Abbey of Arbroath (Aberbro-
thock) in Forfar was founded by King William the Lion
in 1175 with a dedication to St. Thomas Becket, to whose
effective help was attributed the defeat inflicted by
Henry II's army on William 1172, exactly one day after
Henry's penance at Canterbury.   In 1815, there was
discovered in the north-western tower of Arbroath Abbey
a mutilated figure of a mitred ecclesiastic, whose right
hand originally was raised in benediction, whilst his
left hand held the crozier.   This effigy (Plate VI, fig. 4),
a fifteenth-century work displaying much delicacy of
carving, is now set up against the south wall of the
sacristy of the abbey church : it is generally thought to
represent St. Thomas Becket, and this surmise is probably
well founded, since a statue of the saint to whom the
abbey was dedicated is most likely to have existed there.
It has been objected against this identification that the
Bishop has no pallium : but, as we have seen, that
vestment is often missing in representations of the saint.

the Salisbury and South Wiltshire Museum, the Ashmolean
Museum, Oxford, Leicester Museum (a very fine specimen),
Radcliffe College, Exeter, Amport Church, Hants, Lord St. Levan's
collection at St. Michael's Mount, Cornwall, and many other
places.

[1] W. H. St. John Hope, loc. cit., p. 678.

[2] I am indebted to my friend, Dr. W. L. Hildburgh, for making
this very ingenious point.

As one of the very few examples of Gothic figure sculpture on a monumental scale and of fine artistic quality, surviving in Scotland, considerable interest attaches to this work.[1]

In the case of a remarkable piece of German silversmiths' work, dating from 1492, a special mission to England inspired, not inappropriately, the inclusion of a figure of St. Thomas Becket among those portrayed in that work. I am referring to the triptych known as the *Altar der hl. Walburga*, made by the Augsburg master George Seld for Bernhard Adelmann von Adelmannsfelden, Canon of Eichstätt who was sent by the Bishop of that See to England in response to a request of Henry VII for relics of a number of English Saints who repose at Eichstätt. The relics brought by the Canon to the King of England so delighted the latter that he presented the Canon with the sum of 200 crowns ; and on his return to Germany, Adelmann caused this triptych to be fashioned as a thanksgiving for his escape from a gale when crossing the Channel. This exquisite piece now belongs to H.R.H. Crown Prince Rupprecht of Bavaria. On its sinister wing stands, next to St. Barbara, St. Thomas Becket (S. THOMAS MARTIR) shown in high relief as a bishop with crozier and mitre holding the martyr's palm (Plate VI, fig. 6)—a figure marked by that singular elegance which characterizes the entire production.[2]

To other representations of St. Thomas Becket as

[1] I am greatly beholden to my friend Sir Lionel Earle for having this fine piece of sculpture specially photographed for me ; and to Mr. J. S. Richardson for his kind offices in this connection.

[2] I am deeply indebted to H.R.H. Crown Prince Rupprecht of Bavaria for so graciously allowing me to reproduce this item, and for giving me a great deal of detailed information about it. I also have to thank Mr. J. S. Richardson for drawing my attention to this triptych and Mr. F. J. E. Raby, F.S.A., for his erudite remarks on it communicated to me.

archbishop in German sculpture reference will be made further on in different connections.[1]

In Spain, finally, the church of San Tomás Cantuariense in Toro (Province of Zamora), which was in existence by 1208, contains a noble statue of St. Thomas Becket, seated and imparting the Benediction, as the centre of the great *retablo* over the high altar (Plate VI, fig. 5) : it is a work in the style of Berruguete, done shortly before 1550.[2]

St. Thomas as just the archbishop, without any further emblems, also occurs with great frequency among the Canterbury pilgrims' signs, so plentifully represented in the British Museum, the London Museum, the Guildhall Museum and the Royal Museum at Canterbury.[3] A favourite mode of presentment is that of his mitred bust : another is that of the saint on horseback, a motive which probably is not only connected with the fact that the saint was a great traveller, but also reflects his fame as a horseman—there are the accounts of how he fought in Henry II's campaign in

[1] See *postea* p. 62 (Wismar), p. 52 (Brunswick) and p. 68 (Tettens).

[2] See *Catalogo Monumental de España. Provincia de Zamora* (by M. Gomez-Moreno, Madrid, 1927, p. 231, with three plates (275–277), in the companion volume of illustrations.

[3] Compare on these pilgrims' signs, e.g. C. Roach Smith in *Collectanea Antiqua*, Vol. I (1848), pp. 81–91, Vol. II (1852), pp. 43–50 ; T. Hugo in *Archæologia*, Vol. XXXVIII (1860), pp. 128–34 ; H. Syer Cuming in *Journal of the British Archæological Association*, Vol. XXI (1865), pp. 192–6, Vol. XXIV (1868), pp. 219–30. The selection of examples here reproduced has been drawn by Mr. H. C. Whaite, those in the Guildhall Museum being reproduced by kind permission of the Museum authorities. Of individual examples in other collections we may here notice an exceptionally finely modelled bust of St. Thomas between two angels swinging censers, found in the Steelyard, Thames Street, and now in the University Museum of Archæology and Ethnography in Cambridge (Plate XXIX, fig. 3), and an ampulla in the York Museum (reproduced by C. Roach Smith, *op. cit.*, Vol. II, Pl. XVIII).

Southern France and Normandy in 1159, unhorsing, as
Guernes of Pont Ste. Maxence saw him doing, many a
French knight ; and Herbert of Bosham tells us how,

MEDIÆVAL PILGRIMS' SIGNS AND BADGES, IN PEWTER OR LEAD
A. Found in the City of London, Dowgate. Guildhall Museum.
B. British Museum.
C. Cast of Stone Mould. British Museum.
D. British Museum.

after his elevation to the archbishopric, St. Thomas continued to take frequent exercise riding, as he saw no
ascetic reason for giving up that practice.

Mediæval finger rings, engraved with representations
of St. Thomas as the archbishop, are also known : there

are two in the British Museum,[1] both dating from the fifteenth century.

To the seventeenth century belongs a very interesting silver medallion engraved on one side with a bust of St. Thomas Becket as archbishop, on the other with a bust of Sir Thomas More, based upon the famous Holbein portrait. Examples of this counter are now very rare : I know of but three specimens—one in the British Museum (Plate III, fig. 2),[2] and two in the Salisbury and South Wiltshire Museum, but there can be little doubt that it once circulated in large numbers among English Catholics. The juxtaposition of the two characters was suggested, of course, by many analogies existing between them : both were called Thomas, both had been Chancellors of England, and both were put to death by their respective sovereigns—indeed St. Thomas Becket experienced additional ignominy posthumously at the hands of the same King of England who caused Sir Thomas More to be beheaded. This parallel was, so to speak, " in the air " among English Catholics in the sixteenth century : it is elaborated in Nicholas Harpsfield's *Life and Death of Sr. Thomas Moore*, written about 1557,[3] and Thomas Stapleton published in 1558 (at Douai) a book entitled *Tres Thomae* which treats of St. Thomas the Apostle, St. Thomas Becket and Thomas More, who ever since 1572 had, by permission of Pope Gregory XIII, been publicly venerated at the English College in Rome, though he was not

[1] See O. M. Dalton, *Franks Bequest, Catalogue of the Finger Rings* (London, 1912), Nos. 473 and 545 (identity of the figure uncertain in the latter case).

[2] See *Medallic Illustrations of the History of Great Britain and Ireland*, Vol. I (1885), Henry VIII, No. 34, p. 36 (as " Unique ? ").

[3] See the edition of this work by Elsie Vaughan Hitchcock and R. W. Chambers, Early English Text Society (in the press), pp. 214–217. I am much obliged to Prof. Chambers for calling my attention to this passage.

formally beatified until three centuries later—in 1886. The silver medallion referred to, which has a loop for suspension, is in style very closely akin to the medallion of Simon van de Passe, e.g. the well-known counter of James I and Prince Charles.

On monumental brasses in England, figures of St. Thomas as the archbishop are of repeated, if at present not of very abundant occurrence, the most notable examples being perhaps those on the Nelond brass, at Cowfold, Sussex (1453),[1] and at Edenham, Lincs. (c. 1500).[2] In stained glass, such figures are, on the other hand, far from rare in England even now : the absence of any more definite emblem probably acted as a protection in times of iconoclasm.[3]

Next in order of our enquiry come those single figures of St. Thomas in which he is shown with an emblem of

[1] Reproduced in Herbert W. Macklin, *The Brasses of England*, 1913, p. 135.

[2] Compare Mill Stephenson, *A List of Monumental Brasses in the British Isles*, 1926, p. 284 and *passim*, noting additional examples in Hereford Cathedral, at Knebworth (doubtful), and Tattersall (two).

[3] The following is an alphabetical list of localities, in which stained-glass representations of St. Thomas as Archbishop occur at present : it has been drawn up mainly on the basis of Dr. Philip Nelson's *Ancient Painted Glass in England* (London, 1913) and of information supplied by the Rev. George Herbert : Chalvington, Sussex ; Checkley, Staffs. ; Cothelstone, Somerset ; Credenhill, Herefordshire ; Dewsbury, Yorks. (head destroyed) ; Fairford, Glos. (? Window No. 22, Light 3) ; Greystoke, Cumberland ; Hereford Cathedral ; Horton-in-Ribblesdale ; Ludlow, Salop ; Mere, Wilts. ; Norwich, St. Peter Mancroft ; Peover Superior, Cheshire ; Salisbury, St. Thomas of Canterbury ; Thaxted, Essex ; Warwick, Beaufort Chapel (reproduced in the *Birmingham Archæological Society Transactions*, Vol. LIII, 1928) ; Yarnton, Oxon. Not minutely described, but perhaps coming under this head, was the figure of St. Thomas " gloriously painted," which as a result of Henry VIII's edict was replaced in a window in Gray's Inn Chapel by a panel of the Agony in the Garden. (See *Notes and Queries*, October 15, 1887, p. 306.)

his martyrdom. From the circumstances of his death, it is obvious that the sword should be the most natural emblem in that connection. One type—perhaps what might be called the standard type of the martyred St. Thomas—is the one which shows him with his skull cleft by a sword, the latter still adhering to the wound it has inflicted : indeed a rapid sketch of this type came to be used for marking the documents relating to Canterbury in the Exchequer Archives. In English stained glass this type is represented, for instance, in Trinity College Library, Oxford[1] (Plate XIII, fig. 3), in St. Mary Redcliffe, Bristol,[2] and in Minster Lovell Church, Oxon,[3] and in a panel belonging to the present writer ; the Oxford window being at present unique inasmuch as it shows St. Thomas with a mitre *and* the sword in his forehead, while in the other examples he is bareheaded. In the fourteenth-century stained glass in the north-east window of the end of the choir of the Stadtkirche (S. Dionys), in Esslingen in Würtemberg, St. Thomas Becket is described as being represented " as archbishop with his head cleft."[4] On a fifteenth-century ring in the British Museum St. Thomas is seen kneeling, with his sword in his head, before an altar.[5]

[1] The window in question is the third, counting from the door, of the four two-light windows of modest dimensions, containing glass which is surmised to have been originally in the College Chapel.

[2] This is one of a series of fifteenth-century medallions in glass. For indicating this and the next item I am indebted to Mr. G. McN. Rushforth.

[3] The figure is one of two black monks with haloes in the two small lights at the top of the westernmost window on the north side of nave. Minster Lovell had been an alien Benedictine priory before the present church was built *c.* 1430 ; the glass is approximately of the latter period.

[4] See E. Demmler in *Christliches Kunstblatt*, Vol. XLII (Stuttgart, 1900), p. 125 *seq.*

[5] O. M. Dalton, *op. cit.*, No. 720.

Reproductions are here given of two etchings which bring before us late but typical examples of this category (Plate III, fig. 5) ; that on the right being done by W. Hollar in 1647, and according to its inscription reproducing a picture in the Arundel collection, attributed to no less a master than Jan van Eyck. The picture was subsequently in the possession of the Howard family of Greystoke, Cumberland, and was sold some twenty years ago, finding eventually its way to the Metropolitan Museum of Art in New York. It is a small fragment, showing a good deal less of the figure than the etchings : Dr. Friedländer inclines to the opinion that the picture may be the work of the Haarlem mid-fifteenth-century master Albert van Ouwater.[1] In any case, this cannot ever have been an effigy of St. Thomas Becket, for there is no trace of the weapon embedded in the head, and on the shoulder may be seen the hand of another figure : so the inference is that the panel is a fragment of a larger composition, in which some church dignitary was depicted while being introduced to the Virgin and Child by his patron saint.[2]

We may further note that one of the fragmentary panels of fourteenth-century stained glass in Window no. XIV in Fairford Church shows, placed on an altar, a *reliquaire-chef* of St. Thomas with the end of the assassin's sword piercing his head (Plate III, fig. 4). Only one example, associable with England, of this type of the *reliquaire-chef*, so well-known to us, for instance, from the work of the Limoges enamellers, has survived to our day, namely, the fifteenth-century male bust (possibly of Christ), in latten or brass, with traces of silver plating, found near the London Docks at Wapping, and now in

[1] M. J. Friedländer, *Die Altniederländische Malerei*, Vol. III (Berlin, 1921), Pl. XLVII, No. 35, and pp. 61, 112.

[2] See *Archæological Journal*, Vol. XV (1858), p. 165 *seq.* Vorsterman has engraved the same head without the knife also as St. Thomas Becket (Hymans, *Lucas Vorsterman*, Brussels, 1893, No. 88).

the Guildhall Museum.[1]   The principal instance of the
type, so far as St. Thomas Becket was concerned, was,
of course, the one which for many centuries received
the veneration of the pilgrim in the Corona in Canterbury Cathedral, and the aspect of which is perhaps
reflected in some of the Canterbury pilgrims' signs.   To
the iconographic type—exemplified also in a fresco by
Pordenone at Conegliano—showing St. Thomas with
the sword remaining in his head, there exists an
analogy, popularized by many Italian pictures : the
rendering of St. Peter Martyr, the Dominican, who was
murdered on the road between Como and Milan on
April 28, 1252, and canonized the next year.   In his
case the weapon is usually a knife or an axe, not a sword.

The most recent example of this type known to me
from sculpture on a monumental scale, is that occurring
among the nineteenth-century statues, which none too
happily fill a number of niches on the west front of
Salisbury Cathedral.   The sword here cuts into the
mitre of the saint.

Other subsidiary iconographical types of St. Thomas
may now be noted.   One is that of the saint with a
dagger plunged into his heart—as he appears in the
picture of the Virgin and Child with angels and saints,
painted by Felice Brusasorzi (1542–1605) in 1579 for
the high altar of the church dedicated to St. Thomas
Becket in Verona (Plate VII).   Then there is the type
of St. Thomas holding in one hand the archiepiscopal
cross, and in the other an inverted sword, exemplified by
a painting on a tomb in Stoke Charity Church, Hampshire.[2]   Yet another type associated with the sword
as an emblem is that in which it is either placed on

[1] Reproduced in *Catalogue of the Collection of London Antiquities
in the Guildhall Museum*, London, 1908, Pl. LXXXVII, No. 13.

[2] Reproduced in the *Journal of the British Archæological Association*,
Vol. X (1855), Pl. 6, facing p. 74.   (The sword is no longer to be
seen.)

PLATE VIII

PAINTING BY GIROLAMO DA TREVISO (1499–1544),
SAN SALVATORE, BOLOGNA

PLATE IX

PAINTING BY DURANTE ALBERTI (1548–1613)
VENERABLE ENGLISH COLLEGE, ROME

the ground close to the saint, or held by an attendant angel. An instance of the former variant is seen in a picture in the church of San Salvatore at Bologna —a city in which it will be remembered that St. Thomas studied. In this composition the kneeling figure of the saint is, somewhat incongruously, introduced into the foreground of a *Presentation of the Virgin in the Temple* (Plate VIII) : the picture is by Girolamo da Treviso, the artist who eventually entered the service of Henry VIII and was killed by a cannon ball at the siege of Boulogne in 1544. The other variant is seen in the figure kneeling in the foreground on the left, in the picture of the Adoration of the Trinity, by Durante Alberti (1548–1613) in the church of the Venerable English College at Rome (Plate IX). Readers of the delightfully vivid first chapter of Cardinal Wiseman's *Recollections of the Last Four Popes* will remember the reference to this " noble altarpiece " as he calls it—it was that reference which put me on the track of this work—and it is also notable through including a rendering of another English saint, who is much more seldom met with in continental pictures than St. Thomas— namely St. Edmund, king and martyr, killed by the Danes by being shot with arrows—hence the sheaf of arrows held by the angel behind him, while the sceptre on the ground in front of him indicates his kingly rank.[1]

Finally, in modern times, very felicitous use has been made of the emblem of the sword by Mr. George Kruger Gray in a stained-glass window in the church of North

[1] The subject of the Trinity, adored by St. Thomas and St. Edmund, occurs already in an illuminated page in an account book of 1523, belonging to the Venerable College (St. Thomas being here shown with his skull cleft by a dagger), and recurs in an account book of Cardinal Pole's of 1543, also in the possession of the Venerable College. (For this information I am indebted to Mr. Francis Shutt.)

Lew, North Devon. Here the sword is made to pierce, not the head of St. Thomas, but the coat of arms appearing beneath the effigy.

A very interesting variant of the type of the martyred

Wall-painting formerly in the church of Stoke d'Abernon.

St. Thomas is the one which shows him holding in his hand the severed crown of his head. This variant can be exemplified at least twice in England—among the statues on the front of Wells Cathedral[1] (Plate III, fig. 1);

---

[1] Compare St. John Hope in *Archæologia*, Vol. LIX (1904), p. 156, Pl. XXVII ; and W. R. Lethaby, *ibid.*, p. 170 *seq.*

and in the stained glass of the east window of the south aisle at Lincoln. In continental iconography, the renderings of St. Denys and St. Nicaise and some other martyred bishops are somewhat analogous to this variant ; only, of course, they hold their entire heads in their hands, not the crowns only. Yet another variant of the type of the martyred St. Thomas Becket is possibly supplied by a wall-painting which formerly adorned the church of Stoke d'Abernon, Surrey. Here the saint was shown in his archiepiscopal robes, with cross-staff, and on the right, below, a man in armour was depicted in an attitude of supplication. It is of course conceivable that this might be just the figure of a donor ; but it is at least a plausible alternative theory, which sees in the knight one of St. Thomas's murderers ; and a slender connexion between one of them—Richard Le Bret—and Stoke d'Abernon does exist, inasmuch as Stoke d'Abernon stood in some relationship to the Priory of Newark in Surrey (dedicated to Our Lady and St. Thomas of Canterbury), with the endowment of which Richard Le Bret was connected.[1] Hence the possibility that this might have been a composition prompted by an expiatory idea. In the not very accurate reproduction of this wall-painting now available the background is powdered with crescents and stars : this may have been a purely conventional device of ornamental design, though it should be borne in mind that the armorial bearings of Richard Le Bret did include crescents.[2]

[1] See P. M. Johnston, in *Surrey Archæological Collections*, Vol. XX (1907), p. 27 *seq.*

[2] Through the kindness of Mr. P. M. Johnston, F.S.A., I am enabled to reproduce this very interesting painting from a pen-and-ink drawing made about 1866 by an amateur artist, Miss MacGregor. There exists an erroneous statement (repeated in Keyser's *List of Buildings having Mural Decorations*, 1883, p. 239) that the church of Stoke d'Abernon contains a painting of the Murder of

The extraordinarily wide geographical diffusion of
the iconographical material relating to St. Thomas
Becket has already been emphasized : and this point
may be still further illustrated by drawing attention to
a whole group of representations of St. Thomas that
once existed in distant Iceland. Altogether, the interest
that in Iceland was taken in Becket was very remarkable.
I need but recall that we possess—in part or in entirety
—no fewer than three Icelandic *Thomas Sagas*, the
earliest, a fragmentary one, dating from the first half of
the thirteenth century, the complete one a source of the
greatest importance for the history of Becket's life and
work. Indeed, next to St. Olaf of Norway, St. Thomas
was the most popular saint in Iceland : we know of
thirteen churches in the island, dedicated to St. Thomas
singly or jointly ; and effigies (" likneski ") and pictures
(" skript ") of St. Thomas are mentioned in Icelandic
records as having existed in seventeen churches.[1]
Nothing of all this survives, I am sorry to say : at
least there are two mediæval statues of bishops in the
National Museum of Iceland at Reykjavik, but they are
not from churches dedicated to St. Thomas : and in
the country churches I am assured that there are no
representations of him at all.[2] Still, the evidence of the
early records on this point is incontrovertible and I have
thought it worth while to lay stress on the material for

St. Thomas Becket. This is the painting alluded to. As a curiosity
we may here note the representation of St. Thomas as a Bishop
with a Lion in a French Book of Hours, 1490–1500, in the Fitzwilliam Museum at Cambridge (see M. R. James, *A Descriptive
Catalogue of the Manuscripts in the Fitzwilliam Museum*, 1895,
119–53).

[1] See E. Magnússon in the preface to his edition of the *Thomas
Saga Erkibyskups* (Master of the Rolls series, No. 65 ; London,
1875–83), Vol. II, p. 29 *seqq*.

[2] For information on this point I am indebted to M. Mathias
Thórdarson, Director of the National Museum of Iceland.

the iconography of St. Thomas which once was available in the *Ultima Thule*. From the chapels in the Holy Land once belonging to the military order of St. Thomas of Acre, founded in honour of the martyred archbishop a few years after his death, equally interesting material could no doubt have been obtained : but on this point the records are absolutely silent.

Stained Glass Panel ; English, fifteenth century.

CHAPTER III

SERIES OF SCENES FROM THE LIFE OF ST. THOMAS BECKET

FROM the non-narrative representations of the figure of St. Thomas which we considered in the previous chapter we may now turn to the large and important category of renderings of events from his life. Among the fullest series of these now extant is the one to be found in that noble work of English illumination of the early fourteenth century, Queen Mary's Psalter, in the British Museum. No fewer than twenty-two scenes are here represented, the story beginning with the charming and, of course, entirely fanciful story of how the mother of the saint, Mathilde, a Saracen princess, followed Gilbert Becket, the father of St. Thomas, to England, knowing only the words " Gilbert " and " London."[1] The series of incidents is as follows : (1) the Saracen princess arrives in London, jeered at by the crowd and recognized by Richard, the servant of Gilbert Becket (Plate X, fig. 1) ; (2) baptism of the princess ; (3) marriage of the princess and Gilbert Becket ; (4) birth of St. Thomas Becket ; (5) Henry II hands St. Thomas his letters of appointment as archbishop ; (6) St. Thomas consecrated archbishop ; (7) St. Thomas and Henry II disputing (the council at Northampton) ; (8) St. Thomas crossing the Channel

[1] All the illuminations of this MS. have been published by Sir George Warner (*Queen Mary's Psalter*, London, 1912) ; the scenes from the life of St. Thomas Becket, which occur on fols. 288 v–98 v of the manuscript, are given on Plates 282–94 of the volume of reproductions (cf. also p. 50 *seqq.* of the letterpress).

PLATE X

1. ARRIVAL OF THE SARACEN PRINCESS IN LONDON

2. ST. THOMAS CROSSES THE CHANNEL

3. ST. THOMAS AT TABLE WITH THE POPE

4. ST. THOMAS TOLD BY A MESSENGER OF THE
ARRIVAL OF THE FOUR KNIGHTS

ILLUMINATIONS, QUEEN MARY'S PSALTER, BRITISH MUSEUM
EARLY FOURTEENTH CENTURY

(Plate X, fig. 2) ; (9) Henry II pronounces sentence of exile on St. Thomas's relations ; (10) St. Thomas's kindred crossing the Channel ; (11) St. Thomas's kindred travelling on foot ; (12) St. Thomas welcoming his kindred ; (13) St. Thomas handing to Pope Alexander III his ring and cross ; (14) St. Thomas at table with the Pope (Plate X, fig. 3) ; (15) St. Thomas welcomed by the abbot of Pontigny ; (16) St. Thomas has a vision of Christ when praying at an altar ; (17) the reconciliation of St. Thomas and Henry II ; (18) St. Thomas re-crosses the Channel to England ; (19) St. Thomas at table, when a messenger announces the arrival of the four knights (Plate X, fig. 4) ; (20) the martyrdom of St. Thomas ; (21) the burial of St. Thomas ; (22) St. Thomas brought kneeling before Christ in heaven. The subjects of (19) and (20) are, moreover, repeated in a different context in this manuscript.[1]

Even more interesting must have been the series of earlier illuminations of about 1230–50 (possibly of the school of Matthew Paris), illustrating a life of St. Thomas in French verse, of which unfortunately only four pages have survived (Plates XI–XII) : they were in 1883 in the possession of Madame Goethals-Danneel of Courtrai, and in 1885 were published by Monsieur Paul Meyer for the *Société des anciens textes français*. The scenes depicted in these illuminations with great vividness are as follows, in chronological sequence : (1) fol. I r. (*a*) Henry II expelling the friends and relations of St. Thomas ; (2) (*b*) St. Thomas lying ill from too much starvation at Pontigny ; (3) I v. The parting of St. Thomas and Pope Alexander III ; (4) II r. (*a*) St. Thomas pronouncing sentence of excommunication ; (5) (*b*) St. Thomas addressing Henry II and Louis VII of France ; (6) II v. The parting of St. Thomas and the

---

[1] Fols. 236 v, 237. See Warner, *op. cit.*, Plates 242 a and b.

two kings ; (7) III r. (*a*) Roger of York crowning Henry, the king's son ; (8) (*b*) The Coronation Banquet, Henry II serving his son ; (9) III v. The news of the coronation reaches St. Thomas and Pope Alexander ; (10) IV r. St. Thomas embarking for England at Wissant though warned by Milon, Chaplain to the Count of Boulogne ; (11) IV v. St. Thomas landing at Sandwich.

According to Thomas Walsingham the chronicler (c. 1400), Mathew Paris himself wrote and illuminated a Life of St. Thomas Becket ("*Matthaeus Parisiensis vitas SS. Albani, Thome et Edmundi conscripsit et depinxit elegantissime*"). The loss of such a document for the iconography of St. Thomas can never be sufficiently deplored.

The story of the priest who would only chant the Mass of the Virgin and was suspended by St. Thomas, but afterwards, through the intervention of the Virgin, reinstated, is illustrated in the Brailes *Horae* in Mr. Dyson Perrins's collection, in a Bible in the British Museum (I. D. i), and in Queen Mary's Psalter.

Here it may be remarked, incidentally, that an unmistakable affinity exists between the subject matter of this story and one which may be traced back possibly to the first quarter of the thirteenth century and became very popular, notably in Germany and Iceland. It is best known in the version supplied by a curious Middle High German poem (fourteenth century)[1] in which St. Thomas Becket figures as a poor student in Rome. On one occasion when he is merrymaking with eleven companions, it is agreed that each is to produce a precious object belonging to his mistress : he who produces the least valuable object is to pay for the jollification of the company. The poor student whose

---

[1] First published by F. H. von der Hagen, *Gesammtabenteuer*, Vol. III (Stuttgart and Tübingen, 1850), pp. 577–86, and more recently by Richard Scholl, *Thomas von Kandelberg* (Leipzig, 1928), in which the various versions of the legend are fully discussed.

PLATE XI

1. EXPULSION OF ST. THOMAS'S KINDRED—ST. THOMAS
LYING ILL FROM STARVATION

2. PARTING OF ST. THOMAS AND POPE ALEXANDER III

3. ST. THOMAS PRONOUNCING SENTENCE OF EXCOMMUNICATION :
ST. THOMAS ADDRESSING HENRY II AND LOUIS VII

4. PARTING OF ST. THOMAS AND THE TWO KINGS

ILLUMINATIONS, POSSIBLY SCHOOL OF MATTHEW PARIS (1)
C. 1230–50

PLATE XII

1. CORONATION OF HENRY, THE KING'S SON—CORONATION BANQUET

2. THE NEWS OF THE CORONATION REACHES ST. THOMAS AND THE POPE

3. ST. THOMAS EMBARKING FOR ENGLAND THOUGH
WARNED BY THE COUNT OF BOULOGNE'S CHAPLAIN

4. ST. THOMAS LANDING AT SANDWICH

ILLUMINATIONS, POSSIBLY SCHOOL OF MATTHEW PARIS (2)

C. 1230–50

whole mind is given up to the service of the Virgin, receives from her a box, which when opened at the time of the contest is found to contain two church vestments of great beauty. Eventually the Pope appoints the student a bishop ; and the poem ends :

> Von Kandelberch so heizet er
> Sante Thomas von dem ditz mer
> Ist geschriben und gelesen :
> Got gebe daz wir mit im. muezen wesen !

i.e.

> Of Kandelberch so he is called
> St. Thomas of whom this tale
> Is written and read :
> God give that we may be with him.

I am not acquainted with any illustration of this story : unless indeed the famous and puzzling bas-reliefs of subjects from the lives of youthful scholars, on the southern door of Notre Dame in Paris, might have some relation to it.[1]

Elaborate picture chronicles in stained glass devoted to St. Thomas are also extant. In England, the fullest series is that in the magnificent windows of the Trinity chapel of Canterbury Cathedral, dating in the main from the thirteenth century, though considerably restored ; and the triforium windows in the choir aisles also contain stained glass relating to St. Thomas, transferred from the windows of the Trinity chapel. At Canterbury it is, however, now exclusively a matter of posthumous scenes, of miracles worked by St. Thomas after his death and hence interesting the student of the iconography of St. Thomas only somewhat indirectly : though as regards the vexed questions concerning the

[1] For this interesting suggestion I am indebted to Prof. Wolfgang Stammler.

tomb and shrine of St. Thomas these windows yield
information of the greatest value while they also serve
to bring out most effectively what a marvellous micro-
cosm of English mediæval life is contained in these
miracle stories.[1]   Elsewhere in England, fragments
of series, in stained glass, of scenes from St.
Thomas's life as well as of his miracles do survive.   There is
one fragmentary yet fairly extensive series in the north
window of the Chapter House of York Minster (first half
of the fourteenth century).[2]   In the Bodleian Library
there are two fifteenth-century panels, representing
Louis VII welcoming St. Thomas in France and the
Penance of Henry II (Plate XIII, fig. 4), which are
obviously part of a larger series.[3]   The east window
in the chancel of Checkley Church, Staffs, contains,
among others, panels of the Martyrdom of St. Thomas
and the Penance of Henry II ;[4] while the westernmost window on the north side of the nave in Nettle-
stead Church, Kent, contains two subjects connected
with St. Thomas : one of monks welcoming St. Thomas
on his return from exile (inscribed *Voce manu plaudens
patri venit obvia (sc. ecclesia) gaudens*), the other sick
visiting the shrine of St. Thomas (inscribed *Hic jacet
aegorum medicina salus miserorum*, fifteenth century).[5]
The list of surviving examples in England is, it will be

---

[1] For a full description of the glass at Canterbury, see Philip
Nelson, *op. cit.*, p. 109 *seqq. ;* his results are briefly summarized
in Appendix III, *postea*, p. 113.

[2] Compare on this window F. Harrison, *The Painted Glass of
York*, 1927, pp. 52 and 206. For individual panels of stained glass
in York Minster relating to St. Thomas Becket, see *ibid.*, pp. 86 *seq.*,
89, 209, 217.

[3] On these, compare John A. Knowles in *The Bodleian Quarterly
Record*, Vol. V, No. 52, 4th Quarter, 1926, pp. 100–4. The photo-
graph here reproduced has been kindly placed at my disposal by
Mr. Knowles.

[4] Compare Philip Nelson, *op. cit.*, p. 189.

[5] Information received from the Rev. George Herbert. The
second of the Leonine verses quoted above should be compared

noticed, not a long one : before 1538, the position was doubtless quite different, and it has to be borne in mind that iconoclasm was particularly easy when it was a question of stained glass.

In France, on the other hand, the life of St. Thomas figures very prominently to this day among the subjects of some of the finest Gothic stained glass. The cathedrals of Sens, of Chartres and of Angers all contain glorious windows wrought at different dates during the period which extends from the end of the twelfth to the end of the thirteenth century and setting forth at length the varied and dramatic episodes of St. Thomas Becket's life. In a review of the iconography of St. Thomas, these great French Gothic windows should unquestionably hold a central place.

The sequence of subjects in the Sens window (the first in the north ambulatory, date *c.* 1190) is as follows (proceeding from below to the top and from left to right) : (1) reconciliation effected by King Louis VII of France between St. Thomas and Henry II ; (2) St. Thomas landing in England ; (3) entry of St. Thomas into Canterbury ; (4) St. Thomas received by the clergy ; (5) St. Thomas preaching ; (6) St. Thomas saying Mass ; (7) St. Thomas receiving a letter from Henry II ; (8) St. Thomas receiving the king's envoys ; (9) St. Thomas consecrating a church ; (10) St. Thomas confirming ; (11) martyrdom of St. Thomas ; (12) burial of St. Thomas ; (13) Christ receiving the soul of St. Thomas. It will be noticed that the story begins with the departure of St. Thomas from Sens. It has been suggested[1] that another window originally dealt with the earlier part of St. Thomas's life.

with the inscription occurring on a pilgrim's ampulla of which the Guildhall Museum possesses an example :. " *Optimus egrorum medicus fit Toma bonorum.*"

[1] See E. Chartraire, *La Cathédrale de Sens*, Paris, 1928, p. 85, n. 1.

The Chartres window dates from about 1206 ; it was founded by the Corporation of Tanners, and is the fifth window in the *Chapelle des Confesseurs* on the right-hand side of the north transept. The sequence of episodes is as follows : (1) expulsion of St. Thomas ; (2) expulsion of St. Thomas's kindred ; (3) St. Thomas before a king ; (4) St. Thomas on horseback, accompanied by another person arriving at a city gate (there now follow three " signature " panels relating to the Corporation of Tanners) ; (8) consecration of St. Thomas ; (9) St. Thomas addressing Henry II, into whose ear a little devil speaks ; (10) St. Thomas embarks, leaving England ; (11) St. Thomas and Pope Alexander III conversing seated side by side ; (12–13) St. Thomas leaves Pontigny ; (14) St. Thomas converses with King Louis VII of France ; (15) the pope, a king, and St. Thomas (a scene difficult of explanation on strictly historical data, it might be a garbled version of the meeting between the two kings and St. Thomas at Montmirail in 1169) ; (16) St. Thomas recrosses the Channel and arrives at Canterbury ; (17) Henry II talking to one of the bishops inimical to St. Thomas ; (18) refusal of the young King Henry to receive St. Thomas ; (19) St. Thomas conversing with the four knights ; (20) St. Thomas entering the cathedral ; (21) the four knights waiting for St. Thomas ; (22–3) the martyrdom of St. Thomas ; (24–5) scenes round the tomb of St. Thomas.[1] Reproductions are here given of the top portion of this window[2] and of the scene of the murder (Plate XIV, figs. 1–2) which is in this instance combined with a symmetrically arranged scene at the saint's tomb above

[1] In the interpretation of the scenes I have mainly followed the Abbé Y. Delaporte in his volume of text to M. Houvet's photographs of the stained glass at Chartres.

[2] I have to thank M. Etienne Houvet of Chartres for permission to reproduce these illustrations from his admirable photographs of the Cathedral he knows and loves so well.

PLATE XIII

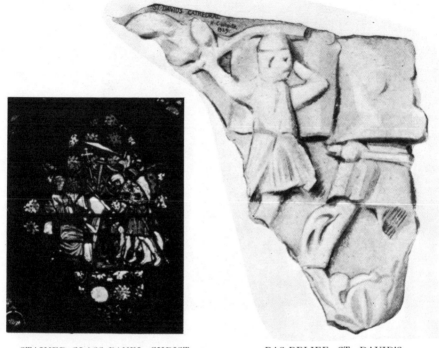

1. STAINED GLASS PANEL, CHRIST
CHURCH CATHEDRAL, OXFORD

C. 1350

2. BAS-RELIEF, ST. DAVID'S
CATHEDRAL

FOURTEENTH CENTURY

3. STAINED GLASS WINDOW,
TRINITY COLLEGE, OXFORD

FIFTEENTH CENTURY

4. STAINED GLASS PANEL, BODLEIAN
LIBRARY, OXFORD

FIFTEENTH CENTURY

PLATE XIV

1. UPPER PART

2. DETAIL, MARTYRDOM OF ST. THOMAS BECKET

STAINED GLASS WINDOW, CHARTRES CATHEDRAL
C. 1206

it, cripples having gathered round the body of the dead martyr ; and this is of particular interest, in connexion with a certain scheme of decoration which we can observe on Limoges *châsses*, and of which I shall have more to say anon.

The window at Angers is the fifteenth of those in the choir, beginning from the first on the north side : building of the choir was commenced in 1274, so the stained glass cannot be earlier than the end of the thirteenth century. The St. Thomas window was restored and in part renewed in 1892 : it contains, apart from four shields of the Beaumont family (commemorating Guillaume de Beaumont, Bishop of Angers 1203–1240), eight medallions with subjects from the life of St. Thomas, which, however, now have got out of their original order. The present sequence is : (1) the three (*sic*) knights meet ; (2) the knights cross the Channel ; (3) Christ appears to St. Thomas (modern) ; (4) the Betrothal of Prince Henry and Princess Margaret of France; (5) St. Thomas remonstrating with Henry II ; (6) St. Thomas as a boy saved from drowning in a millstream (the incident referred to previously and mentioned by various early writers, but, so far as I am aware, nowhere else illustrated) ; (7) death of St. Thomas (modern) ; (8) burial of St. Thomas (largely restored).[1]

As to later French stained glass, it may be noted that to the fourteenth century belong the remnants of a series of the life of St. Thomas in the church of Saint Ouen at Rouen.[2] The subjects occurring in this window, which is the second of the ambulatory (counting from the north

---

[1] Compare Joseph Denais, *Monographie de la Cathédrale d'Angers*, Paris, 1899, pp. 449–51 ; Ch. Urseau, *La Cathédrale d'Angers*, Paris, 1930, p. 62 *seq.* I am indebted to Miss Mary Chamot for drawing my attention to this window.

[2] Cf. André Masson, *L'Eglise Saint Ouen de Rouen*, 1927, p. 78.

transept) are : St. Thomas before King Henry II ; the break between the archbishop and the king ; martyrdom of St. Thomas.

Turning now to wall-paintings of a series of successive incidents from the life of St. Thomas, the first example of this category takes us to Spain. As to the veneration of St. Thomas in Spain it may be remarked by way of introduction that it doubtless received a strong stimulus from the marriage of Eleanor, daughter of Henry II, to Alfonso III of Castile. The Norman-born Queen founded " about 1174 " a chapel dedicated to St. Thomas in Toledo Cathedral—the site of this chapel is now occupied by the Capilla de Santiago ; and another chapel was dedicated to St. Thomas in the cathedral of Sigüenza by Bishop Jocelyn who accompanied the Princess Eleanor to Spain. In Salamanca there exists to this day the extremely interesting little Romanesque church of San Tomás Cantuariense from which, however, all traces of the representation of the saint have vanished, except a very commonplace painted statue of a mitred archbishop with crozier and book, of fairly recent date. We hear of an altar to St. Thomas in Barcelona Cathedral in 1186[1] ; and perhaps from the very end of the twelfth century—in any case from a period not very distant from the year 1200—dates one of the most notable items bearing on the iconography of St. Thomas —the series of wall-paintings in the church of S. Maria

[1] At Aviles, on the Cantabrian sea coast, there is in the suburb of Sabuga a church dedicated to St. Thomas of Canterbury concerning which I know nothing, except that Richard Ford in his guidebook to Spain advises one to look at it ; of the dedication of a church to St. Thomas at Zamora shortly after his death I only know just the fact (see E. S. Dodgson in Notes and Queries, July 9, 1904, p. 32). Of the church of Toro which was in existence by 1206 I have already spoken (p. 28). In one of the stained-glass windows of León Cathedral (central window of the Capilla de la Consolacion in the Ambulatory) I thought I saw one panel which might represent the Murder of St. Thomas.

at Tarrasa, in the Carlist country about fifteen miles due north of Barcelona.

The church in question was consecrated in 1112 ; and the paintings which interest us in the first instance are those which adorn the apse of the right transept. They were discovered some fifteen years ago[1] and were then on the whole, save for one or two large breaks, in very good state of preservation : I understand that they have since been somewhat ruthlessly repainted. The paintings occupy two tiers (Plate XV, fig. 1). In the lower one we see depicted three successive scenes from the life of St. Thomas. First, beginning from the left, the interview between St. Thomas, accompanied as usual by Edward Grim, and the knights, three in number, who assume either a threatening or mocking attitude (Plate XVI, fig. 2). There follows the scene of the murder (Plate XV, fig. 2) : St. Thomas has been seized from behind by one of the attackers : another stands on the left, with his sword raised ; but the deathblow is being dealt by a figure on the extreme right, and with such tremendous force that his sword is bent[2] : the mitre and the crozier of the archbishop meanwhile falling to the ground. Third follows the scene of the burial of the saint, whose soul is being carried heavenwards by two angels—a symmetrically disposed scene akin to those which occur on numerous Limoges *châsses*.

Above the tier now described, in the semidome of the apse, we see in the centre Christ enthroned within a

---

[1] See José Soler y Patel in *Museum*, Vol. V (Barcelona, 1917), p. 295 *seqq.*, with reproductions. These paintings have subsequently been discussed by C. R. Post, *A History of Spanish Painting*, Cambridge, Mass., 1930, pp. 149–51 and Fig. 25 ; and by Charles L. Kuhn, *Romanesque Mural Painting of Catalonia*, Cambridge, Mass., 1930, p. 41 *seq.* and Plates XXXV–VII. I am indebted to Mr. Eric P. Barker for first drawing my attention to these paintings.

[2] Unless indeed the sword is one of a particular type with curved blade.

4

mandorla, the seven candlesticks of the Apocalypse being placed on the strip of ground ; and Christ, assuming a hieratic, symmetrical attitude, is touching the heads of two figures with books. Of these the figure on the left (Plate XVI, fig. 1) is quite obviously the archbishop. The figure on the right was interpreted by Senor Soler y Patel as Edward Grim, and he has been followed in this by everyone who has up to now written on these paintings. It would, however, be absolutely unexampled to promote to such an exalted position the clerk from Cambridge who happened to be at Canterbury in December 1170, and who, it is true, stood by St. Thomas very bravely during the great struggle of which he has left a long account and in the course of which he had one of his arms almost severed. I feel personally no doubt that the only possible interpretation of the figure on the right is one that has been suggested to me by my friend Mr. Hedley Hope-Nicholson—namely, that he must be St. Stephen, the proto-martyr, whose feast occurs but three days before that of St. Thomas. Indeed, we have seen that in the wall-paintings on the ceiling of the vaulting of the Relic chamber at Norwich, about a century later than those at Tarrasa, St. Thomas Becket and St. Stephen are represented standing next to each other[1] ; and on two embroidered mitres (at Munich and Sens)[2] while the martyrdom of St. Thomas appears on the front, that of St. Stephen appears on the back : so there was evidently a tendency to bracket the two martyrs whose feasts are so near to one another.

The story of the murder is told at Tarrasa with a certain freedom—one point to be noted is that there are only *three* knights present. This, however, is not an unusual feature, and is probably due to the fact that one of the four, Hugh de Moreville, took no active part in the

[1] See *antea*, p. 18.   [2] See *postea*, p. 83 *seq.*

PLATE XV

2. MARTYRDOM OF ST. THOMAS BECKET

1. ENTIRE APSE

WALL-PAINTINGS, S. MARIA, TARRASA (1)
C. 1200

PLATE XVI

1. DETAIL OF SEMI-DOME

2. THE KNIGHTS MOCKING ST. THOMAS

WALL-PAINTINGS, S. MARIA, TARRASA (2)

C. 1200

slaying of the archbishop, but stood all through the scuffle at the entrance of the transept, keeping intruders away. There need, in fact, be no hesitation on the evidence of the paintings alone, in accepting the identification of the saint with St. Thomas Becket ; and in addition, in the unfortunately fragmentary inscriptions which run below the lower tier there occurs repeatedly the word THOMAS—once in the context " THOMA BO . . ." once, as I interpret it, (THO)MAS QUEM SEMPER AMAVIT.[1] The character of this lettering indicates the very end of the twelfth or the beginning of the thirteenth century as the date of the paintings—a dating borne out also by the style of the paintings, which show the characteristic rude force of the Catalan wall-paintings of this period. We are, I may add, always perhaps disinclined to give the Middle Ages sufficient credit for their gradual extension of the subject matter of painting beyond the time-honoured sacred themes. Still, in much ecclesiastical painting, convention was clearly supreme : and we can therefore appreciate what a relish of actuality, of topicalness, the painter must have derived from a contemporary subject like this.

The next example of a surviving series of early wall-paintings illustrating the life of St. Thomas Becket occurs

[1] This phrase suggests the end of a hexameter, and if so can only have a very vague general relationship to any verses in an office of St. Thomas. Mr. Hope-Nicholson has drawn my attention to the second Antiphon of the second Nocturn at Matins of the Feast of the Translation of St. Thomas :

Thomas coram Domino
Vixit in timore
Ideo cum Domino
Regnat cum decore

(Sarum Breviary, British Museum, Sloane MSS., 1909, fol. 374 v.). These words are, as a matter of fact, singularly appropriate to the scheme of the Tarrasa paintings, even if—apart from other considerations—it has to be borne in mind that the Feast of the Translation was not instituted until 1220.

in Germany : and again we find how the worship and representation of the saint followed in the wake of a daughter of Henry II married abroad.

This most remarkable picture chronicle forms part of the extensive scheme of wall-decoration, carried out in the first half of the thirteenth century, in the cathedral of Brunswick—a church which stood in a particularly close relationship to the veneration of St. Thomas Becket. It was consecrated in 1226, on December 29, the day of St. Thomas, who had been made one of the patron saints of the cathedral by Heinrich of Brunswick, called " der Pfalzgraf," whose mother, Matilda, was a daughter of Henry II of England ; so there was an association with St. Thomas Becket on two counts—the tie of relationship with Henry II on the one hand, and the Guelph that is pro-papal tendencies of the House of Brunswick on the other. In consequence, representations of St. Thomas Becket are of frequent occurrence in Brunswick.[1]

The paintings in Brunswick Cathedral were, unfortunately, very drastically repainted in the last century ; but even so, they remain of the utmost interest and importance. The scenes from the life of St. Thomas (Plate XVII, fig. 2) occupy a long frieze-like space on the south wall of the choir, underneath two similar friezes containing scenes from the lives of St. John the Baptist

[1] Compare in addition to the wall-paintings in the cathedral, the engraved fourteenth-century back of a reliquary in the now scattered Welfenschatz, containing three patron saints of the cathedral, namely, St. John the Baptist, St. Blaise and St. Thomas Becket (reproduced in W. A. Neumann, *Der Reliquienschatz des Hauses Braunschweig-Lüneburg*, Vienna, 1891, p. 17 ; and in *Der Welfenschatz*, Frankfurt, 1930, Plate 83) ; a silver book-cover of 1326 decorated with bas-reliefs, also in the Welfenschatz, on which St. Thomas Becket is one of five saints surrounding the Virgin and Child (reproduced in W. A. Neumann, *op. cit.*, p. 241 and *Der Welfenschatz*, Plate 75) ; two statues in the St. Aegidienkirche ; the late fourteenth-century altarpiece in the choir of the Minderenkirche (Brüdernkirche) ; and the seal of the diocese of St. Blasien, of about 1338 (cf. W. A. Neumann, *loc. cit.*).

and St. Blaise. Seven scenes are represented, but of these only the four first are old : as to the three others, nothing of the original compositions remaining when the work of restoration was taken in hand, the restorer Heinrich Brandes has put it on record that he had to invent three further subjects himself, so as to complete the series.[1] Even in the first scene, representing the crowning of St. Thomas as archbishop in the presence of Henry II, the lower half of the composition is entirely new : but here the restorer had, of course, ample data to go by. There follows the scene of St. Thomas disputing with Henry II, the subject being probably intended for the Council of Northampton (October 1164) seeing that the next scene shows St. Thomas escaping on horseback. The fourth scene shows a king, no doubt Henry II, addressing a group of people. We need feel no hesitation in recognizing here a rendering of the occasion when sentence of exile was pronounced upon the relatives of St. Thomas, after his flight to France—such a scene does occur among the illuminations of the Goethals-Danneel manuscript and Queen Mary's Psalter,[2] and the fact of this ferocious

[1] See his little book *Braunschweigs Dom mit seinen alten und neuen Wandgemälden* (Brunswick, 1863), p. 14.

[2] In this connexion it may be noted that the early biographers of Becket give an account of the hospitality extended to these exiles, thanks to the intercession of the archbishop, in various parts of Europe, but notably in Sicily ; and indeed all over Italy there exist families claiming descent from St. Thomas Becket's relatives. The inscription on the tomb of a member of the Becchetti family, in the church of S. Tommaso Cantuariense at Verona, is worth quoting in the present context :

TUO HOC IN TEMPLO /CANTUARIENSIS ANTISTES,/THOMA SANCTE / AGNOSCE, ET ACCIPE,/TUUM CERTUM GENUS/IO BAPTISTAM BECHETUM FABRIANUM,/HONORATISS. HOMINEM /HIERONYMUS ALBERTUS F. MARTYR /MOERENTES FILII MOERENTES /FECERE /MOERENTI PATRI MOERENTI / SIBIQUE, SUISQUE /.

See G. B. Cola, *Vita di S. Tomaso Arcivescovo di Cantuaria e Martire*, Lucca, 1696, p. 179.

reprisal is mentioned in the Service on St. Thomas's Day. Here follow the three scenes devised by Brandes, the number probably corresponding to that of the original series : and the final scene was no doubt also in the original version, the Martyrdom, so the inventive powers of the restorer were chiefly exercised in the two preceding scenes. He has shown St. Thomas kneeling before Pope Alexander III at Sens—not a bad shot iconographically—and the Reconciliation of Henry II and St. Thomas at Fréteval in Normandy (July 1170). Of this scene there does exist a rendering in the Sens window : another and perhaps more likely alternative is that of the Return of St. Thomas from exile.

Although unfortunately thus mutilated and drastically restored, these wall-paintings at Brunswick must rank among the most important documents for the iconography of St. Thomas. It appears *a priori* unlikely that there should exist no parallel to this series anywhere ; for we can scarcely imagine that it does not reflect an iconographical tradition which by that time had obtained a wide diffusion. Indeed a series of late Romanesque wall-paintings of the second half of the thirteenth century, now lost but until the sixties of the last century partly visible in the Nicholas Choir of the Cathedral of Trier, very likely illustrated the life of St. Thomas Becket by means of an even larger number of scenes than at Brunswick. That, at least, may not improperly be deduced—as Professor Wolfgang Stammler has suggested to me—from the (not very accurate) drawings after these lost paintings which have been preserved.[1] The subjects have been interpreted as relating to the legend of St. Lambert of Liége but they lend themselves undoubtedly much better to an identifi-

[1] See P. Clemen, *Die Romanische Monumentalmalerei in den Rheinlanden*, Dusseldorf, 1916, pp. 621–623.

PLATE XVII

1. ST. MARY'S CHURCH, STOW, LINCS.
EARLY THIRTEENTH CENTURY

2. BRUNSWICK CATHEDRAL (VERY MUCH RESTORED)
FIRST HALF OF THIRTEENTH CENTURY

WALL-PAINTINGS

PLATE XVIII

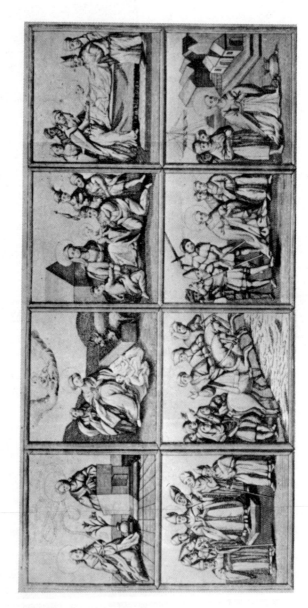

ENGRAVING DATING FROM 1731 OF THE *THOMASALTAR*, BY MEISTER FRANCKE
1434

cation with incidents from the life of St. Thomas Becket. No fewer than ten scenes are depicted, namely :

1. Henry II appoints St. Thomas Archbishop.
2. St. Thomas consecrated Archbishop in the presence of Henry II.
3. St. Thomas washes the feet of the poor (according to his biographers he washed the feet of thirteen poor men daily : the scene occurs in the fifteenth-century altarpieces at Wismar and Tettens of which more anon).
4-5. Exile and Return of St. Thomas Becket.
6. St. Thomas told by a Heavenly messenger of his impending martyrdom.
7-8. Story of the Priest suspended from saying mass, who gave St. Thomas a message from the Virgin about his hair shirt.
9. The Knights arrive at Canterbury Cathedral.
10. Martyrdom of St. Thomas.

If the interpretation here put forward be accurate, the importance of St. Thomas Becket for the iconography of Romanesque wall painting in Germany would indeed be brought most vividly into relief.[1]

As to English mediæval painting there is not very much that is tangible that can be quoted in the way of instances of several scenes from St. Thomas's life being depicted on church walls. That such scenes existed in England one may, I think, assume *a priori* ; and there

---

[1] It may be noted that a series of thirteenth-century frescoes, in the chapel known as the " grotta di San Tommaso " in the cathedral of Anagni, may have illustrated the life of St. Thomas Becket. At least this is the reference to them in Signor Toesca's paper in *Le Gallerie Nazionali Italiane*, Vol. V (1902), p. 182 : " Sul muro di fronte sono affrescate alcune storie ora troppo deperite perchè se ne possa facilmente riconoscere il soggetto : forse esse si riferiscono a San Tommaso, chè nell' ultima scena appaiono soldati irrompenti con le spade sguainate in un tempio mentre la turba del popolo fa gesti d'orrori."

are even certain vestiges of them to which one may point
with some degree of certainty. There is, for instance,
the case of the two bands of paintings above the sup-
ports of the altar of the FitzHamon Chantry at Tewkes-
bury, built in 1397. The very faint traces of paintings
here to be seen a close examination indicates with great
probability as representing a succession of scenes from
the life of St. Thomas, beginning with his coronation
as archbishop, including further on a scene in which he
appears on horseback, and ending up with his martyrdom.[1] Moreover, there is the possibility that a series
of scenes from the life of St. Thomas once was to be seen
on the wall of the south aisle of the church of Merstham,
Surrey, where a very faint figure of St. Thomas, painted
on the west pillar of the south side of the nave, can still
be made out blessing those entering the church (somewhat like "Becket's ghost" in the crypt at Canterbury).
Traces of paintings were discovered in 1861 along the
whole wall of the south aisle, but were subsequently destroyed : among them the most distinct figure is said to
have been a man drawing his sword, and the suggestion
that this was a fragment of a scene of the Martyrdom of
St. Thomas was an obvious one, seeing that Merstham lay
on one of the direct routes of the pilgrims to Canterbury.[2]

Again, there is a suggestion as to the existence in
England of a series of subjects from the life of St. Thomas,
which has been assigned to the thirteenth century.[3] The
paintings in question surround the former altar of St.

---

[1] I have to thank Miss Eleanor Hollyer for her kind offices in
deciphering the remains of these paintings.

[2] Compare Alfred Heales in *Surrey Archæological Collections,*
Vol. III, p. 7 *seq.*

[3] The suggestion referred to is the following statement in
Mr. Keyser's *List of Buildings having Mural Decorations,* 1883, p. 282,
under " Chapel of the Hospital of St. Cross " : " S. transept.
E. Wall : within an arched recess, the Crucifixion ; and above,
under a series of trefoil-headed arches, events in the life, and the
martyrdom of St. Thomas à Becket. 13th cent."

Thomas Becket in the south transept of the church of the Hospital of St. Cross in Winchester, but all that now can be deciphered of these paintings is a fragment of the scene of the murder, and reasons of space preclude the possibility of the series ever having been an extensive one.

Then we can actually point to the existence of wall-paintings of *two* scenes of Becket's life—the murder and the repast which preceded it—flanking a figure of the saint (Plate XVII, fig. 1), in St. Mary's Church, Stow, Lincolnshire[1] : a group of early thirteenth-century paintings of very considerable interest—as the Rev. George Herbert points out—from various historically very accurate details in the scene of the martyrdom. Thus, St. Thomas is shown wearing a canon's cloak (*cappa*), not a chasuble, as in most representations of the murder ; and on the right is seen the column near which he was slain, and which was pulled down not very long after the event.[2] Finally, my investigations in the church at Bramley, Hampshire, point to the possibility that originally there was yet another scene from the life of Becket on the left of the fine painting of the Martyrdom of which I shall have more to say anon.

Coming now to a series of several panel pictures relating to the life of St. Thomas Becket, I know of three instances where two or more pictures survive, all associated with Germany, though of considerably later date than the Brunswick wall-paintings. The earliest of these

[1] An account of these wall-paintings, which were uncovered in 1866, and now, as Mr. P. M. Johnston tells me, are very greatly faded, is given in the *Associated Architectural Societies Reports and Papers*, 1866, Vol. VIII, Part II, p. 249 *seq.*, together with a woodcut, from which our reproduction is taken.

[2] In conformity with the parallel established between the Martyrdom of St. Thomas and the Passion of Christ the repast of St. Thomas here depicted might have been made to correspond with the Last Supper : but I know of no early authority for such a parallel. St. Thomas at table, receiving the news of the arrival of the knights, is represented in Queen Mary's Psalter (Plate X, fig. 4).

series forms part of one of the most notable productions
of German fifteenth-century painting—the altarpiece
dedicated to St. Thomas Becket, which Meister Francke
of Hamburg in 1424 undertook to paint for the Hamburg Confraternity of the " Englandsfahrer," or mer-
chants trading with England.   From a very inaccurate
engraving (Plate XVIII) dating from 1731,[1] we know
that the wings of this altarpiece, the *Thomasaltar* as it
is called, when closed displayed eight pictures, viz. four
from the life of the Virgin and four connected with St.
Thomas Becket.   These latter scenes were : (1) the enthronement of St. Thomas ; (2) the mob insulting St.
Thomas ; (3) the murder of St. Thomas ; and (4) a
scene representing a man—evidently a king, and with a
halo—kneeling in a harbour city, before a royal crown
placed on a cushion.   Of these four pictures only two
survive, in the Hamburg Museum, namely, the second
and the third subject.   In the one which chrono-
logically comes first (Plate XIX, fig. 1), what we see
is St. Thomas, with two companions on horseback,
jeered at by a mob, one man of which has cut off
the tail of St. Thomas's horse.   The artist has here
depicted an incident, connected by popular tradition with the town of Strood, near Rochester, where
the people insulted Becket as he rode through the
town by cutting off the tails of his horses.   For this,
tradition has it that the descendants of the people who
did it were punished by being ever after born with
horses' tails ; indeed there is a tradition traceable in
Spain that *all* Englishmen, but especially the inhabitants
of Kent, are born with tails for curtailing Becket's mule.
Concurrent with this story is the account handed down
by William FitzStephen, that right at the end of St.
Thomas's life, after his return to England—on Christ-

[1] Nicolaus Staphorst, *Historia Ecclesiæ Hamburgensis*, Part I,
Vol. IV (Hamburg, 1731), plate facing p. 64.

PLATE XIX

1. THE MOB INSULTING ST. THOMAS BECKET

2. THE MARTYRDOM OF ST. THOMAS BECKET

PICTURES FROM THE *THOMASALTAR*, BY MEISTER
FRANCKE (1434), KUNSTHALLE, HAMBURG

PLATE XX

1. THE MARTYRDOM OF ST. THOMAS BECKET

2. THE FUNERAL OF ST. THOMAS BECKET

PAINTINGS OF THE SCHOOL OF MICHAEL PACHER
MUSEUM, GRAZ

mas Eve, 1170, to be quite accurate—Robert de Broc, a relative of the archbishop's particular enemy Ranulph, sent out his nephew John to waylay and cut off the tail of a sumpter-mule and a horse belonging to St. Thomas. It may be noted that this particular insult weighed heavily on St. Thomas's mind. He spoke of it in his Christmas Day sermon and he referred to it in his last interview with his murderers, shortly before the tragedy : " They have attacked my servants, they have cut off my sumpter-mule's tail, they have carried off the casks of wine that were the King's own gift."

The other picture of this series by Meister Francke, which has come down to us (Plate XIX, fig. 2), is of a much more familiar subject—the martyrdom of St. Thomas : and I think it cannot be gainsaid that it is the finest pictorial interpretation which has been inspired by this oft-repeated scene. Iconographically the composition is of considerable interest, inasmuch as it shows *three* of the archbishop's friends present—a number which, as we shall see, is quite accurate in the sense that three of his friends actually witnessed the beginning of the tragedy. This feature, taken together with the inclusion of the rarely represented scene of the mob insulting St. Thomas (concerning which the *Golden Legend* is silent) points to very accurate information concerning the life of the archbishop having been possessed by the person who set the subjects for the *Thomasaltar*, and the considerable familiarity with Canterbury affairs is further disclosed by the fourth picture in the series, now lost. Of this scene, a very convincing interpretation was first suggested by Dr. Alfred Lichtwark[1] and has recently been elaborated by Fräulein Bella Martens.[2] The King kneeling in a harbour city must be Becket's friend the pious King Louis VII of France, who among his many

---

[1] Alfred Lichtwark, *Meister Francke*, Hamburg, 1899, p. 125 *seq.*
[2] Bella Martens, *Meister Francke*, Hamburg, 1929, p. 216 *seq.*

pilgrimages made a famous journey to St. Thomas's tomb, crossing the Channel in 1179; and the halo round his head springs probably from a confusion with *Saint* Louis—Louis IX—the best known of the French mediæval Louis of kingly rank. The pilgrimage of Louis VII was, as M. Jusserand[1] has well expressed it, " a prodigious and unparalleled event, the first time a king of France had ever set foot on British soil. Feeling that for him death was near, and having had, although three times married, only one son, he decided in 1179 to have the young prince crowned at once, but before the ceremony, Philip, aged fourteen, while boar hunting, lost his way in the forest of Compiegne, and, separated from his companions, endured for days such hardships before a charcoal-burner found him and led him out of the maze that his life was despaired of. The King, in his anguish, had at night a vision of St. Thomas Becket, whom he had well known, promising life for his son if he himself went to Canterbury as a pilgrim. Louis' advisers recommended not to risk a journey which would place him at the mercy of his enemy, the Plantagenet king. But again, and yet again, St. Thomas appeared at night, now threatening disaster. Louis started then with a brilliant retinue, and no untoward event marred the journey. Henry II, on the contrary, very meek now when his former chancellor was in question, came to meet the French monarch at Dover; both went together to Canterbury; Louis remained two days in prayer, and offered the monks a gold cup and a magnificent gem shown henceforth to pilgrims as the ' regale of France.' By a special charter he granted them, besides, one hundred casks of wine to be taken yearly for ever, at vintage time, from his cellars of Poissy-sur-Seine. He returned to find his son on the way to recovery;

[1] J. J. Jusserand, *English Wayfaring Life in the Middle Ages*, London, 1925, p. 353 *seq.*

and, having had him crowned, died within a year." Little wonder, then, that this great and outstanding event in the long series of Canterbury pilgrimages should have been thus specially commemorated in the *Thomasaltar*.

Considerably later than the Hamburg series are a couple of scenes painted by an artist of the school of the great Tyrolese master Michael Pacher (died in 1498) on the outer sides of two panels (nos. 24, 25) in the museum at Graz. The subjects depicted (Plate XX) are the Murder of St. Thomas and the Funeral of the saint In the former scene, three knights and several witnesses of the event are introduced ; the funeral takes place in the cathedral, with several people present and some angels descending from heaven. The subjects were as a matter of fact at one time interpreted as scenes from the life of a Polish saint, St. Stanislaus Szepanow of Cracow, who censured the conduct of Boleslaw, King of Poland, so energetically that he had to flee : the emissaries of King Boleslaw overtook him, however, in the church of St. Michael in Cracow, and slew him in the year 1079, as he was celebrating Mass. It will be seen that this story would fit the Graz pictures equally well : but they illustrate the life of St. Thomas all the same and the proof of this is the fact, but recently discovered, that they originally formed part of an altarpiece in the church of Neustift, near Innsbruck, and that the chapel which contained the altarpiece was dedicated, among others, to St. Thomas of Canterbury.[1] Various circumstances make it indeed probable that

[1] Compare on this discovery, by Prince Josef Clemens of Bavaria, Eberhard Hempel, *Michael Pacher*, Vienna, 1931, p. 81 *seq*. Dr. Elisabet Valentiner has kindly called my attention to a drawing of 1511 by Hans Süss von Kulmbach, in a private collection in Germany, evidently a design for stained glass, where a crowd is breaking into a church and the foremost figure attacks a bishop celebrating Mass. I should not like to affirm that this drawing

there originally were *two* altarpieces in the chapel, and that the two Graz panels are the only survivors of a series of *eight* scenes from the life of St. Thomas Becket.

Whilst the Hamburg and Neustift altarpieces have thus not come down to us in their entirety, the third series to which I referred is absolutely complete. It occurs on the wings of an altarpiece of the late fifteenth century, dedicated to the three St. Thomases—St. Thomas the Apostle, St. Thomas Becket and St. Thomas Aquinas —in the church of St. Jürgen at Wismar in Mecklenburg. When opened (Plate XXI) the altarpiece contains in the centre three figures in carved wood of the three saints—St. Thomas Aquinas in the centre, on the left of him the Apostle, and on the right St. Thomas Becket, in bishop's robes, mitred, holding the crozier and a model of a church ; the bas-reliefs on the wings represent scenes from the life of St. Thomas Aquinas. When the outer wings are opened, and the inner wings closed, each wing contains four scenes from the life of a saint, that on the left St. Thomas the Apostle, that on the right St. Thomas Becket (Plate XXII), namely (1) the enthronement of St. Thomas, who in the background is washing the feet of the poor ; (2) Henry II driving St. Thomas into exile—in the background, on the left, he is kneeling before the Pope at Sens, while on the right is probably seen, somewhat cryptically rendered, the episode at Strood ; (3) St. Thomas accompanied by two ecclesiastics ; in the background, the story of the priest suspended from saying Mass ; (4) Louis VII of France at Canterbury ; in the background the Martyrdom.

A curious fact in this connexion is that, so far as I know (and I have also consulted Dr. Friedländer on the point) there exists no Early Flemish pictures either of

represents the Martyrdom of St. Thomas Becket : on the contrary, I incline to think that it is connected with the story of St. Stanislaus Szepanow.

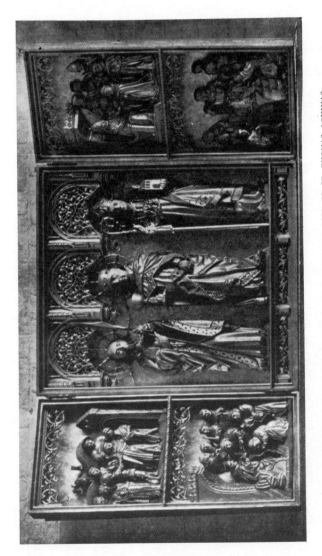

PLATE XXI

THE THREE ST. THOMASES AND SCENES FROM THE LIFE OF ST. THOMAS AQUINAS

ALTARPIECE, ST. JÜRGEN, WISMAR (1)

LATE FIFTEENTH CENTURY

PLATE XXII

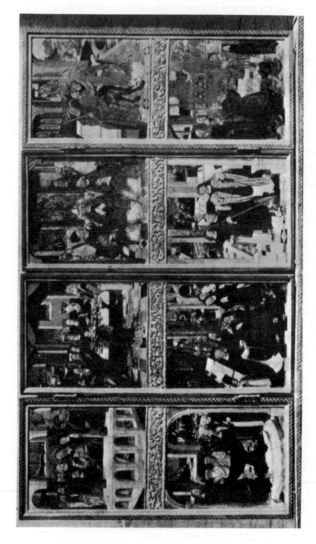

SCENES FROM THE LIVES OF ST. THOMAS THE APOSTLE (LEFT) AND ST. THOMAS BECKET (RIGHT)

ALTARPIECE, ST. JÜRGEN, WISMAR (2)

LATE FIFTEENTH CENTURY

the life of St. Thomas Becket or of a single incident of it. There is a picture in the collection of the Duke of Devonshire, famous in the annals of art-history on account of the forged inscription it once bore, purporting that it was a work by Jan van Eyck. This picture used to be interpreted as the enthronement of St. Thomas Becket, but it is now with greater reason and doubtless rightly regarded as representing the enthronement of St. Romold, archbishop of Dublin.[1] It belongs to a series illustrating the life of the latter saint, of which the greater part is still in the church of St. Rombaut at Malines, the very church in which according to one legend the four knights who slew Becket were buried, having in the course of a pilgrimage eventually regained their lost senses of taste and smell, the former at Cologne, the latter at Malines.

As to English mediæval panel pictures, I can point to one example associable with England which probably represents a scene from the life of St. Thomas Becket and obviously is one of a series. This is a panel which was shown at the British Primitives Exhibition and now belongs to Mr. Francis Harper of Bickleigh Castle, Tiverton.[2] All that I have been able to ascertain concerning the provenance of this picture is that it is said to have come from a church in East Anglia : as to the date, it is obviously the second half of the fifteenth century. The subject lends itself well to being interpreted as an interview between Henry II and St. Thomas : and it may be noted, that the presence of the soldiers on the left is in conformity with the iconography adopted for the rendering of the Council at Northampton in the alabaster table in the church of Elham in Kent.

[1] See *Catalogue of the Loan Exhibition of Flemish and Belgian Art, Burlington House, London (Memorial Volume)*, 1927, No. 129, p. 156.

[2] Reproduced in *Archæologia*, Vol. LXXXI, Pl. XX, fig. 1.

Passing on to Italian painting of a much later time, it should be noted that in the Western part of Padua there stands the church of San Tommaso Cantuariense which contains a group of works by Italian seventeenth-century masters which form quite an interesting province of the later iconography of the saint. Two of them are companion pieces, being canvases of enormous dimensions. One (Plate XXIII, fig. 2) represents the Virgin, accompanied by a large retinue of angels, appearing to St. Thomas kneeling at the foot of an altar in a church, looking up from a book on a book-rest before him ; in the foreground child angels are playing with his mitre and patriarchal cross. This picture is by Pietro Liberi (1605–1687), famous during his lifetime as a painter of nudities which earned him the sobriquet of *il Libertino*. The companion picture, by the little-known painter Onofrio Gabriello (1616–1706), known as Onofrio da Messina, is a very populous composition, showing Christ surrounded by angels, appearing to St. Thomas Becket in a vast hall crowded with ecclesiastics and other figures : an angel descends towards St. Thomas, with the palm of martyrdom and a wreath of flowers. Both works—enlarged in the eighteenth century by the addition of several figures by F. Zannoni—are typical creations of the Venetian Baroque, following in the wake of Tintoretto if *longo intervallo* : the age was that of visions and apparitions as favourite painters' subjects, and the artists have given free reins to their pictorial rhetoric in presenting scenes for which only one, as far as I know, possesses an iconographic precedent— namely, Christ appearing to St. Thomas, a subject occurring also in Queen Mary's Psalter. The subject of the Martyrdom is also present in the Paduan church, through a picture by Giovanni Battista Pellizzari (Plate XXIII, fig. 1) of Verona, a not ineffective composition, in which the aged archbishop, kneeling in the

PLATE *XXIII*

1. PAINTING BY G. B. PELLIZZARI

2. PAINTING BY PIETRO LIBERI

SAN TOMMASO CANTUARIENSE, PADUA

PLATE XXIV

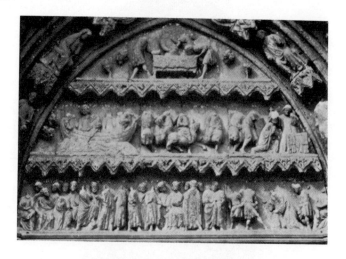

1. TYMPANUM, BAYEUX CATHEDRAL

LATE THIRTEENTH CENTURY

2. RELIQUARY, HEIDAL, VALDRES, NORWAY

C. 1250

centre, is being attacked by two dashing cavaliers, Grim watching the scene a little further back : above is a representation of the Trinity, and an angel descends towards St. Thomas with the crown and palm of martyrdom.

Turning from painting to sculpture, the first thing to be noted is that France can show an elaborate chronicle of St. Thomas's life in stone in the late thirteenth-century bas-relief above the gate of the southern transept of the cathedral of Bayeux (Plate XXIV, fig. 1). An interpretation of the scenes which are represented in three tiers is rendered somewhat difficult by the mutilation which many of the figures have suffered ; but we have in all probability here : (1) the council at Northampton, and next to it the arrival of St. Thomas in France, greeted by King Louis VII ; above this (2) St. Thomas crossing back to England, proceeding on horseback to Canterbury, and being murdered ; and at the top (3) a scene at the tomb of St. Thomas.

In England, a strangely haphazard selection of scenes connected with St. Thomas Becket occurs among the subjects sculptured on the bosses of the cloisters of Norwich Cathedral. The Becket subjects are to be found in the North Alley which is stated to have been completed in 1430 : it is a matter of six bosses in the eighth bay, including the large central boss representing the four knights, inspired by two demons, about to attack St. Thomas, kneeling at the altar, with Edward Grim and an angel behind and to the left of him. Elsewhere on the vaulting are represented the Penance of Henry II ; the opening of the tomb of St. Thomas (?) ; the Burial of St. Thomas ; the Penance of Henry II once more ; the Slaying of St. Thomas.[1]

[1] Compare on these bosses M. R. James, *The Sculptured Bosses in the Cloisters of Norwich Cathedral*, Norwich, 1911, p. 26 *seq.* and Plate VIII.

The Norwich bosses make up the most complete series of sculpture connected with St. Thomas Becket surviving in England. On the double piscina in the chapel of St. Thomas Becket in St. David's Cathedral, there occurs a fine bas-relief (Plate XIII, fig. 2) of two figures fighting, protected by rectangular shields such as were used in ordeals by battle : it is just possible that this may refer to the miracle worked by St. Thomas in helping a weaker combatant to overcome a stronger one during a trial by ordeal : though the description of the incident[1] has little resemblance to the scene represented at St. David's.

As to English alabasters, there is, of course, a strong probability *a priori* that many series of subjects of the life of St. Thomas existed in this medium. Actually, two companion tables exist, which undeniably represent scenes from the life of St. Thomas ; they are in the collection of Dr. Walter L. Hildburgh (Plate XXV). These two tables are of very considerable interest, being both artistically of very fine quality and also iconographically notable : especially that which represents the landing of St. Thomas Becket at Sandwich on his return from exile. This is a subject which may be taken as indicative of the feast of the *Regressio Sancti Thomae ;* it is so far unparalleled among English alabasters, but not in other artistic mediums : it occurs for instance in Queen Mary's Psalter and in the fragmentary series of earlier illuminations, possibly of the school of Matthew Paris, which in 1883 were in private hands in Courtrai.

The fact that this bas-relief thus indubitably represents a scene from the life of St. Thomas Becket, allows us to conclude that the accompanying bas-relief does represent the audience granted to St. Thomas Becket at Sens by Pope Alexander III, after St. Thomas had escaped from England : a scene with which a bas-relief

---

[1] See Edwin A. Abbott,. *St. Thomas of Canterbury*, London, 1898, Vol. I, p. 324.

in St. Mary's, Nottingham, had hitherto been but tentatively identified[1]—the subject is one which also occurs in the Tettens altarpiece, to be mentioned presently, the Wismar altarpiece and elsewhere. How many tables the altarpiece to which these two belonged originally comprised, is impossible to say : among the fairly numerous surviving alabasters representing different scenes from the life of St. Thomas there is none which on grounds of size and style may be associated with them. As to these other alabasters, I may note that the Martyrdom of St. Thomas Becket is represented on four alabaster panels which have come down to us—on this point further details are given in the next chapter.[2] The council at Northampton is represented on an alabaster table in Elham Church, Kent.[3] There are, moreover, in existence alabaster panels, such as the two in St. Louis-en-l'Isle in Paris, representing the birth and burial of an archbishop[4] and one in Dr. Hildburgh's collection, representing the consecration of an archbishop,[5] all of which might and very probably do represent scenes from the life of St. Thomas Becket, even if we cannot at present definitely assert this.

From the domain of German mediæval sculpture there are finally to be quoted two late Gothic altarpieces with

[1] P. Nelson in *Archæological Journal*, Vol. LXXV, 1918, p. 332, and Plate XXIV. Here the scene is interpreted as more probably representing St. William of York before Pope Eugenius III on the slender ground that Nottingham formed part of the diocese of York : but the composition is so analogous to that of Dr. Hildburgh's panel, that there can be no doubt that the Nottingham panel also represents St. Thomas before Alexander III.

[2] See *postea*, p. 81 *seq.*

[3] See *Illustrated Catalogue of the Exhibition of English Medieval Alabaster Work, Society of Antiquaries*, 1913, No. 39, Plate XVIII ; and P. Nelson in *Transactions of the Historical Society of Lancashire and Cheshire*, 1917, p. 87 ; see Plate VII.

[4] See P. Nelson, *loc. cit.*, p. 89 *seq.*, and Plate IX.

[5] See W. L. Hildburgh in *The Antiquaries Journal*, Vol. I, 1921, p. 227 *seq.*

wood carvings, both of them again taking us to the
North German seaboard. The more remarkable of the
two is that which belongs to the church of Tettens in
Oldenburg (Plate XXVI, fig. 1). In the centre is the
Crucifixion, flanked by figures of St. Thomas Becket and
St. Martin of Tours : and six scenes from the legend
of each saint have been represented on the inside
of the wings. These have got out of their original
order, the correct sequence on the St. Thomas wing
being : (1) the Consecration of St. Thomas ; (2) St.
Thomas feeds the poor and washes their feet ; (3) St.
Thomas kneels before Pope Alexander III at Sens ; (4)
St. Thomas rides through the town of Strood, near
Rochester, and the mob insult him by cutting off his
horse's tail—the same subject as occurs in the *Thomasaltar* at Hamburg ; (5) the Murder of St. Thomas—
he is being slain by only one knight ; (6) Henry II
doing penance at the tomb of St. Thomas Becket. It
will be admitted that this elaborate series of subjects
throws vividly into relief the interest taken in St. Thomas,
in Northern Germany. In particular is it interesting to
find here, as in Hamburg, and probably also at Wismar,
the scene of the insult offered St. Thomas by the mob at
Strood, which, as I have already remarked, is unknown
to the *Golden Legend* and of which no rendering survives
in England.[1]

The other of the altarpieces referred to was originally in
the church of St. Nicholas at Stralsund, where ever
since 1304 there had existed a *Vicarie* of St. Thomas
Becket. In 1618, this altarpiece was sold to the church
of Waase, a village on the island of Ummanz, in close
proximity to the island of Rügen : and in this in-
accessible locality the altarpiece has remained to this

[1] For information about this altarpiece I am much beholden
to Pastor Hans Thorade of Tettens, a keen student of the cult and
iconography of St. Thomas Becket in Germany, and to Dr. Müller-
Wulkow, Director of the Landesmuseum in Oldenburg.

PLATE XXV

1. ST. THOMAS BECKET RECEIVED BY
POPE ALEXANDER III

2. THE RETURN OF ST. THOMAS
BECKET

ALABASTER TABLES, DR. WALTER L. HILDBURGH

FIFTEENTH CENTURY

PLATE XXVI

I. TETTENS

2. WAASE (DETAIL)

ALTARPIECES

FIFTEENTH CENTURY

day.[1] The lower of the two tiers of subjects represents the following scenes : (1) dexter wing, Consecration of St. Thomas Becket ; (2) centre : Murder of St. Thomas Becket (two knights, Grim and other figures are present) (Plate XXVI, fig. 2) ; (3) sinister wing—a scene difficult of interpretation : an old man in armour who, attacked by two knights, has fallen on his knees ; in the background other figures. One wonders whether this scene could be a garbled version of the Penance of Henry II.[2]

[1] E. von Haselberg, *Die Baudenkmäler des Regierungs-Bezirks Stralsund*. Heft IV (Stettin, 1897), p. 359.

[2] For a photograph of the central subject I am indebted to Prof. Otto Schmitt of Greifswald. Two German centres of the cult of St. Thomas Becket may here be mentioned : the Liebfrauen-kirche in Halberstadt, where an altar was consecrated in the Chapel of St. Thomas in 1396 ; and the church dedicated to him at Merseburg, which is first mentioned as far back as 1188. In neither church do any representations of St. Thomas Becket now survive.

CHAPTER IV

SINGLE REPRESENTATIONS OF THE MARTYRDOM
OF ST. THOMAS BECKET

IF, as we have seen, the whole of the life of St.
Thomas Becket was regarded as a subject well
worthy of artistic representation all over Europe,
there was, however, one incident in his life—the Martyrdom—upon which, for obvious reasons, attention in the
first instance centred. Individual representations of the
Martyrdom—at times supplemented by renderings of
the burial and the reception of the saint in Heaven
—are hence of great frequency : and it is interesting
to note that this episode also used to be enacted as
a pageant, at Canterbury and elsewhere.[1] Before
we go on to examine the single representations of the
murder of St. Thomas existing all over Europe, I
may perhaps be allowed to recall a few of the salient
facts connected with it.

When in the afternoon of December 29, 1170, the
four knights—Reginald Fitzurse, Hugh de Moreville,
William de Tracy and Richard Le Bret—arrived at the
archbishop's palace at Canterbury, they first laid down
their swords, and then entered the hall of the palace
where the servants were partaking of the remains of the

---

[1] On these pageants, see Thomas Wright, " On the Municipal
Archives of the City of Canterbury," in *Archæologia*, Vol. XXXI,
1846, pp. 207–9 (the date of the earliest pageant mentioned being
1504), and Dean Stanley, *Historical Memorials of Canterbury*, London,
1875, p. 223, n. 2 (noting performances on the Eve of St. Thomas,
at the chapel of St. William of Norwich on Mousehold Heath).

dinner served to the archbishop at three o'clock. With
the knights was an archer named Ralph. The four
were then shown into the room to which the archbishop
had withdrawn : and there followed a discussion in
which Becket would make no concessions as regards the
points at issue. Feeling soon ran very high on both
sides : and the knights eventually left the palace, calling
out as they did so, " To arms, to arms." They now
picked up their swords, and the door of the hall having
been bolted, Robert de Broc, who had meanwhile
appeared on the scene, took the knights up a staircase
known to him in the archbishop's palace. They thus
again obtained access to the hall, but were unable to
enter the archbishop's room : in mounting the staircase
they had picked up an axe and some hatchets, left behind
by some workmen who had been repairing the wooden
steps of the staircase.

Whilst this was happening, Becket—after a brief conversation with his friend John of Salisbury, who tried
to exercise a moderating influence—had decided to pro-
ceed to the cathedral where the vesper service was about
to begin. His cross-staff was borne before him by a
clerk called Henry of Auxerre. Amid the terror of the
other ecclesiastics, Becket showed no sign of waning
courage, preserving his calm and dignity unimpaired.
Advancing through the cloisters, he eventually reached
the door of the north transept, and having entered the
cathedral, noticed that the door behind him had been
shut and bolted, from fear of the knights and their
adherents, who by now had found their way into the
cloisters and were approaching the door through which
Becket had passed a few moments before. The archbishop with his own hands threw the door open, and
there now followed a general *sauve qui peut* in the cathedral—the vesper service had already previously been
abruptly broken off. Becket alone together with three

faithful adherents—his old teacher Robert of Merton, William FitzStephen and Edward Grim—would not seek safety in flight or hiding : the most he would do was—yielding to his friends' entreaties—to ascend the steps leading up to the choir, there to await events.[1]

Meanwhile the four knights had entered the church, and with them was one Hugh of Horsea, a degraded clerk : behind the group followed a knight called Robert Fitzranulph and three others, while still further back was a miscellaneous crowd of " King's men " (*reaux*). The active part in the dramatic scene which was to ensue belonged, however, entirely to the first group, and here Reginald Fitzurse was the leader, entering the cathedral ahead of the others, sword in one hand and the carpenter's axe in the other. " Thomas Becket, traitor to the king," having been called for by the invaders, the archbishop answered them with great dignity from the steps to the choir which he was then ascending : he thereupon descended into the transept and here eventually the actual struggle (in which Becket at first gave a very good account of himself, far back though his athletic days then lay) took place between a pillar and the wall forming one of the corners of the chapel of St. Benedict. It is somewhat difficult to reconcile the accounts of the various writers of what happened after St. Thomas, resigned to his fate, gave up all resis-

---

[1] John of Salisbury, it may be noted, had deserted him by this time ; though at a later stage of the conflict, Tracy mistook Edward Grim for him. The authority for the latter statement is Guernes of Pont Ste. Maxence (VV. 5596–5600) :

> A Saltwode sont li fellin returné
> De lur grant felunie se sunt la nuit vanté ;
> Vuillaumes de Traci a dit et afermé
> Johan de Salesbire aveit le braz colpé :
> Par çosavum qu'il eut maistre Eduvard nafré.

(See the edition of Guernes' *Life of St. Thomas*, by Prof. E. Walberg, Lund, 1922, p. 189.)

tance, commending his cause and that of the Church
to God, St. Mary and St. Denys. Dean Stanley interprets the information thus : Fitzurse, having discarded
his axe, was the first to strike a blow with his sword :
this, however, only dashed off St. Thomas's cap. Tracy
was the first to wound St. Thomas, though the force of
the blow dealt by him was partly spent by descending
upon the arm of Edward Grim who, alone of the three
who were with the archbishop in the choir, stood by
him at this moment and did his best to protect him :
only then did Grim, with his arm almost severed, with-
draw from the scene. Dr. Abbott, on the other hand,
accepts as likeliest the version that it was Fitzurse who
both struck off the cap of the archbishop, and wounded
his skull besides injuring the arm of Grim. The *last* blow
—which severed the crown of St. Thomas's head—was
delivered by Richard Le Bret, whose sword broke in
two on striking the pavement ; the fragments of his
weapon were subsequently preserved on the simple
wooden altar set up in the transept in the year 1172,
when the cathedral was again open to worship—the
altare ad punctum ensis, the altar of the sword-point, as
it was called.[1] After St. Thomas had been slain, it was
—on the evidence of a majority of writers—Hugh of
Horsea who, taunted by the others with his inaction,
put his foot on the neck of the archbishop and scattered
his brains on the pavement.

It is scarcely necessary to emphasize that at no time
after the irruption of the knights was St. Thomas praying
at an altar, let alone saying Mass : though this is suggested by most representations of the murder, with an
evident intention of laying a melodramatic stress on the
horror of the scene and the enormity of the sacrilege.
That Edward Grim carried the cross-staff of the arch-

[1] The traces of this altar, pulled down in 1538, can still be
made out on the floor of the transept.

bishop is, so far as I can make out, first stated in the thirteenth century by Jacobus de Voragine in the *Golden Legend* and again in the next century by John Grandisson, Bishop of Exeter, the devotee of St. Thomas for whom the two ivory triptychs in the British Museum were made. That Grim acted thus appears indeed not unlikely ; though at an earlier stage of the proceedings, it was, as we have seen, Henry of Auxerre who acted as cross-bearer to Becket. As to what the latter wore on this occasion, we are told it was a white rochet with a cloak and hood over his shoulders.

The list of the different categories into which the single representations of the martyrdom fall is in itself a lengthy one. We have to deal with seals, pilgrims' signs in lead and pewter, other metalwork, sculptures in stone, ivories, stained glass, embroideries, woodcuts, enamels, illuminations, easel pictures and wall-paintings.

The extensive and interesting category of seals is of particular importance inasmuch as it includes the earliest more or less definitely datable representation of the murder : namely, the counter-seal of Hubert Walter, archbishop of Canterbury between 1193 and 1205 (Plate XXVII, fig. 1). The composition includes two murderers and Grim.[1] Next follows the counter-seal of Stephen Langton (archbishop 1207–28),[2] with *four* murderers and a dove descending from above (Plate XXVII, fig. 2); while the counter-seal of Richard Grant of Wethershed (archbishop 1229–31) introduces a composition in two tiers (Plate XXVII, fig. 3) : above in the principal compartment a scene of the martyrdom with four murderers, below a very curious and indeed so far as I am aware unique feature : the heads of the horses of the four knights, held

---

[1] See W. de G. Birch, *Catalogue of Seals in the Department of MSS. in the British Museum*, Vol. I (1887), No. 1187.

[2] Birch, *op. cit.*, No. 1196.

PLATE XXVII

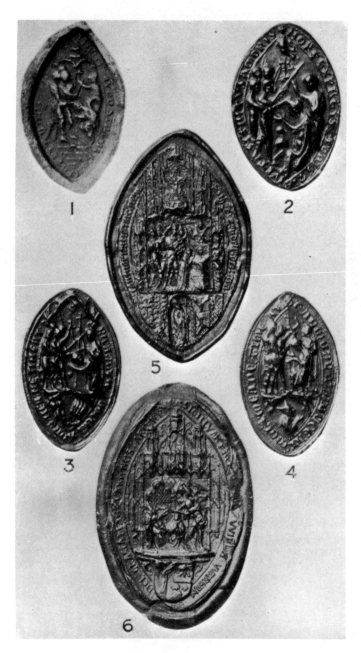

1. COUNTER-SEAL OF HUBERT WALTER, ARCHBISHOP OF CANTERBURY
1193–1205
2. COUNTER-SEAL OF STEPHEN LANGTON, ARCHBISHOP OF CANTERBURY
1207–28
3. COUNTER-SEAL OF RICHARD GRANT, ARCHBISHOP OF CANTERBURY
1229–31
4. COUNTER-SEAL OF ST. EDMUND RICH, ARCHBISHOP OF CANTERBURY
1233–40
5. SEAL OF THOMAS ARUNDEL, ARCHBISHOP OF CANTERBURY, 1397–1419
6. SEAL OF THE PREROGATIVE COURT OF ARCHBISHOP WARHAM, 1504–23

PLATE XXVIII

7. SEAL OF THE PREROGATIVE COURT OF CARDINAL POLE
1555–8
8. SEAL OF THE PREROGATIVE COURT OF ARCHBISHOP CRANMER, *SEDE VACANTE* DURING HIS IMPRISONMENT
1553–5
9. SEAL OF ARBROATH ABBEY, FORFAR
THIRTEENTH CENTURY
10. REVERSE OF THE THIRD SEAL OF THE CATHEDRAL PRIORY OF CANTERBURY
1233

by two men.[1] In the counter-seal of St. Edmund Rich of Abingdon (1233-40) this feature is replaced by a half-length profile of the archbishop praying (Plate XXVII, fig. 4).[2] Though there are many variations in detail, this became the standard type for the seals of the archbishops of Canterbury for quite a long time : of later examples, I reproduce (Plate XXVII, fig. 5) the fine seal of Thomas Arundel (archbishop 1397-1414).[3] The seal of the Prerogative Court of Archbishop Warham (1504-32) shows a particularly dramatic scene of the murder in which St. Thomas is kneeling facing the spectator and the coat of arms of the archbishop replaces the figure of the bishop below (Plate XXVII, fig. 6). Two kindred post-Reformation examples here reproduced are the seal of the Prerogative Court of Cranmer, *sede vacante* (1553-5) during the imprisonment of the archbishop (Plate XXVIII,fig.8); and the seal (Plate XXVIII, fig.7) of the Prerogative Court of Cardinal Pole (1555-8), in both of which the scene of the murder—after its excision in the seals of the archbishops of Canterbury and elsewhere —reappears. A particularly interesting seal iconographically is the reverse of the third seal of the Cathedral Priory of Canterbury, made in 1233 (Plate XXVIII, fig.10) in which the scene of the murder is displayed in four arcades of the front of the cathedral : in the centre, two murderers, St. Thomas, and Grim, on the left two more murderers, on the right two friends of St. Thomas—a very unusual feature.[4] Outside Canterbury there would be a number of interesting seals to quote ; considerations of space prevent me from referring to more than two,

[1] *Ibid.*, No. 1201, misinterpreting the horses as " shields " (?). The correct interpretation has been pointed out to me by Mr. H. S. Kingsford, to whom I am much indebted for information regarding seals bearing on the iconography of St. Thomas Becket.

[2] *Ibid.*, No. 1202.　　　　[3] *Ibid.*, No. 1238.

[4] *Ibid.*, No 1373. The friends of St. Thomas are here misinterpreted as knights.

the fine thirteenth-century seal of Arbroath Abbey, Forfarshire[1] (Plate XXVIII, fig. 9), and that, belonging to the same century, of the Priory of St. Mary, Langdon, Kent, of which the bronze matrix exists in the British Museum.

Of pilgrims' ampullæ in pewter or lead, containing representations of the murder, a considerable number of varieties exist. Five selected types are reproduced in the accompanying illustrations from the examples in the Guildhall Museum and the British Museum. In the Musée de Cluny there is a notable example, from the Victor Gay collection, showing the murder and another scene with St. Thomas seated, mitred, and addressing some clerics.[2]

Of the examples of other metalwork, much the most notable is, I think, the fine reliquary in the church of Heidal, Valdres, Norway (Plate XXIV, fig. 2), in all probability the work of a Norwegian craftsman of about 1250.[3] The accuracy of the representation here is considerable : there are five assailants, which is correct if we add Hugh of Horsea to the number ; on the archbishop's side there are three people present ; the archbishop's cap is shown falling to the ground, and the sword of one of the assailants breaks as he strikes the archbishop's head. Grim is represented carrying the archbishop's cross-staff which, as we saw, may or may

[1] It may here once again be recalled that Arbroath Abbey was founded by King William the Lion of Scotland whom the army of Henry II defeated and took prisoner at Alnwick the day after Henry II's penance at Canterbury.

[2] Reproduced in V. Gay, *Glossaire Archéologique*, Vol. I, p. 30.

[3] I am indebted to Dr. Haakon Shetelig for supplying me with the photograph from which the reproduction is made, and for drawing my attention to the fact that this châsse and other examples of kindred character in Norway have lately been discussed by Dr. Thor Kielland, *Norsk Guldsmedkunst i Middelalderen*, Oslo, 1921, pp. 97–115. An electrotype of this shrine may be seen in the Victoria and Albert Museum.

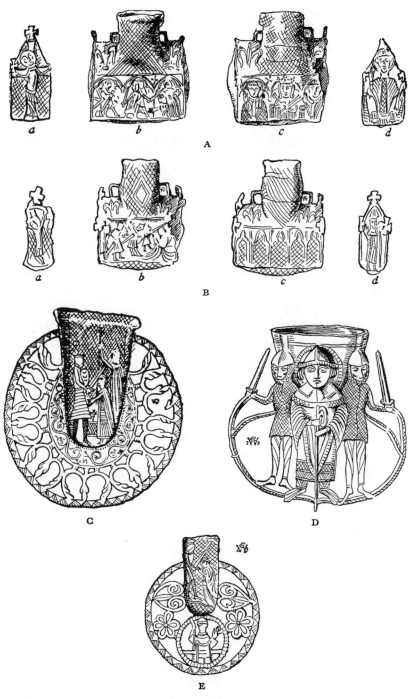

A, B. Reliquaries in form of a shrine, found in the City of London
Steelyard. Guildhall Museum.
C—E. Ampullæ, British Museum (Fig. D somewhat reconstructed).

not be accurate, but had in any case by this time become
the tradition—a tradition indeed, as we saw, incor-
porated in the *Golden Legend*. On the other hand the
altar with the chalice and the dove of the Holy Ghost
gives that suggestion that Mass was being said, which
is a very frequent, but historically quite inaccurate,
feature in these representations.

Under the heading of metalwork we have further to
notice a very interesting tiny reliquary of silver with
niello decoration of very fine quality, in the Metropolitan Museum of Art in New York. The suggestion
has been made concerning this reliquary[1] that it was
once in the possession of John of Salisbury, Becket's
friend who was present at any rate at the beginning of
the conflict with the murderers.[2] It is on record that
he collected some drops of St. Thomas Becket's blood
in two vials which he gave to the cathedral of Chartres,
of which he became bishop in 1176, dying in 1180 :
previously, between 1174 and 1176 he had been treasurer of Exeter Cathedral. The interior of the reliquary
originally contained a thin partition, so two vials could
have found place inside it. As to the exterior, it contains niello plaques in all the four divisions of the lid
(which is surmounted by a ruby) and all four sides of
the box. The niellos which principally interest us are
those on the front and back of the box. There is comparatively little to be said of the front (Plate XXIX, fig. 1)
on which St. Thomas Becket receives the death blow

---

[1] See Joseph Breck in the *Bulletin of the Metropolitan Museum of Art*, Vol. XIII (October 1918), pp. 220–24.

[2] Guernes of Pont Sainte Maxence has recorded, as already mentioned, that William de Tracy was under the impression that the monk wounded by him was John of Salisbury. The latter, however, undoubtedly deserted the archbishop already some time before the struggle began ; and it is perhaps indicative of a feeling of embarrassment on his part that in his own account of the murder he does not mention the heroism of Grim.

PLATE XXIX

3. PILGRIM'S SIGN, MUSEUM OF ARCHÆOLOGY, CAMBRIDGE

FIFTEENTH CENTURY

1. THE MURDER OF ST. THOMAS BECKET

2. THE BURIAL OF ST. THOMAS BECKET

SILVER RELIQUARY WITH NIELLO DECORATION, METROPOLITAN MUSEUM OF ART, NEW YORK, LATE TWELFTH CENTURY

PLATE XXX

1. CEILING BOSS, EXETER CATHEDRAL
FOURTEENTH CENTURY

2. FONT, LYNGSJÖ, SWEDEN
1190-1200

3. BAS-RELIEF, NORTH DOOR
CHARTRES CATHEDRAL
C. 1250

from the foremost of the three knights—s. TOMAS OCCIDIT as the inscription explains. On the back (Plate XXIX, fig. 2) is the burial—two figures of ecclesiastics carrying St. Thomas to the grave : and here the interpretation of the inscription raises a very interesting problem. Mr. Breck reads it

IT SANGUIS E(xcelsi) S. TOM(ae) E

and interprets the first two letters as " Iohannes Terserarius " indicating John of Salisbury at the time when he was treasurer of Exeter Cathedral ; while to him " E " stands for " Edwardus " (Grim). As against this, my friend Mr. Francis Wormald has put forward the following interpretation

(H)IC SANGUIS E(st) S(ancti) TOM E

and I own that both on paleographical and general grounds such an interpretation strikes me as being preferable. It is of course perfectly possible that this is the reliquary that once belonged to John of Salisbury : but the reliquary itself, I fear, hardly supplies quite as explicit evidence in favour of that possibility as Mr. Breck thinks. I must not, however, leave this reliquary without still further emphasizing the high rank which it takes artistically, through its style of figure drawing in the noblest late Romanesque style. It is not easy to determine its place of origin : if it had been done, as Mr. Breck suggests, during John of Salisbury's tenure of office at Exeter, it would of course have been almost inevitable to regard it as of English origin, and the possibility that it was done in England is even now not to be excluded.

That the martyrdom of St. Thomas sometimes was represented on the " prints " (i.e. niello or translucent enamel plaques) occurring at the bottom of mazers may be seen from this entry in the Inventory of the goods of the Guild of the B. V. Mary of Boston, taken in 1534 :

Itm̃ a masar wȋ a sengle band wȋ a prynt in the bothom of the passion of saynt Thomas the martir & a plate of sylu' & gilte wȋ an Ape lookynge in an vrynall written wȋ these woordes " this wat' is polows " weynge xv vnces di.[1]

Of sculpture in stone, Scandinavia offers an example (Plate XXX, fig. 2), which is very notable for one thing on account of its date, which has been put as early as 1190–1200 : it occurs on a font in the church of Lyngsjö in the Province of Skåne in Southern Sweden.[2] The representation here actually begins with the interview between Henry II and one of the knights ; then another is seen hurrying away ; and finally two are seen attacking the archbishop in the presence of Grim ; the chronicle of the event being rounded off by the reception of the saint in heaven. The presence of this subject on a Scandinavian font is all the more remarkable as no parallel to it exists on any English font.

At Chartres, among the bas-reliefs of the north Door (c. 1250) we see a representation of the murder, with only two assailants present (Plate XXX, fig. 3) ; and France can also offer, in the sixteenth-century church of Saint-Thomas-de-Cantorbéry in Landerneau (Brittany), two early eighteenth-century bas-reliefs of scenes from St. Thomas's martyrdom (together with a fine statue).

In England the subject was repeatedly represented in the bas-reliefs of ceiling bosses—I have already

[1] Edward Peacock, *English Church Furniture . . . at the Period of the Reformation* (London, 1866), p. 195.

[2] Compare Lars Tynell, *Skånes medeltida dopfuntar* (Stockholm, 1913), p. 33 *seq.*, and Plate VIII, 1–2. See also Romilly Allen in *The Reliquary*, 1906, pp. 126–31. The photograph here reproduced has been most kindly placed at my disposal by Professor Otto Rydbeck of Lund.

referred to the two in the cloisters of Norwich Cathedral,[1] there is one instance in Chester Cathedral, and a particularly fine one at Exeter (Plate XXX, fig. 1), in which the full normal complement of actors in the drama is seen—four knights and Grim.[2] The subject also occurs in the much decayed late fifteenth-century bas-reliefs on the tower of the church of St. Mary at Burnham Market, Norfolk,[3] and in one of the equally weather-worn bas-reliefs, of the same century, occupying one of the faces of the interesting sculptured base of the ancient stone cross at Rampisham, Dorset.[4]

Of alabaster panels the number must originally have been very large, though I only know of four surviving examples; one in the British Museum (Plate XXXI, fig. 1), one in the possession of Mr. F. J. Foljambe,[5] one in the Rouen Museum,[6] and one in the collection of Mr. Frank J. Gould (this last dated 1460).[7] Of these, that belonging to Mr. Foljambe is historically the most interesting, since it is supposed to come from Beauchief Abbey, Derbyshire, which according to tradition was founded by Robert Fitzranulph in expiation of the part—not a very active one—which he took in the murder of St. Thomas. The three coats-of-arms sculptured at the

[1] See *antea*, p. 65.

[2] For the excellent photograph from which this reproduction is taken I have to thank Mr. C. J. P. Cave, F.S.A.

[3] Compare on these the Rev. T. Felton Falkner in *Norfolk Archæology*, Vol. XVII (1910), p. 277 *seqq.*

[4] I have to thank Mr. Philip Johnston, F.S.A., for drawing my attention to this work.

[5] Reproduced in the *Illustrated Catalogue of the Exhibition of English Medieval Alabaster Work, Society of Antiquaries*, 1913, Plate XXVIII.

[6] Reproduced in P. Nelson, " Some Unusual English Alabaster Panels," in *Transactions of the Historical Society of Lancashire and Cheshire*, 1917, p. 80 *seqq.*, Plate VII, 3.

[7] Reproduced in P. Nelson, "Some Unpublished Alabaster Carvings," in *The Archæological Journal*, Vol. LXXXII, Plate X, 1, facing page 34.

bottom of the panel are : (1) gules, six fleurs-de-lis or for Ireland ; (2) Foljambe (sable a bend and six escalops or) impaling Ireland ; and (3) Foljambe. These arms belong to Sir Godfrey Foljambe who married as his second wife Avena, daughter of Sir Thomas Ireland, and died in 1376, his wife surviving him until 1382.

As to ivories, I know of five examples, all dating from the fourteenth century : two in the Victoria and Albert Museum (Plate XXXI, figs. 2 and 3), one in the Figdor collection, Vienna,[1] one in the late Homberg collection (sale in Paris, 1908, no. 486) (Plate XXXI, fig. 4),[2] and one in the Fitzwilliam Museum at Cambridge, McClean Bequest, no. 41.[3] It is, of course, not a large number ; but relatively not inconsiderable if one bears in mind how very rarely subjects from the lives of the saints occur on ivories of this period.[4]

In the category of stained glass the most interesting single example known to me as extant is the octofoil panel in a window of the east wall of the chapel of St. Lucy, in the south transept of Christ Church Cathedral, Oxford (Plate XIII, fig. 1). The vividly dramatic composition is effectively silhouetted against a background of curvilinear diaper in red and blue. The head of St. Thomas is missing, the glass having obviously been broken in that place, in obedience to Henry VIII's order of 1538. Grim is present, and the number of the knights is four : the shields of three of them are visible, being blazoned :

First knight : or, three bears' heads sable. (Le Bret.)

Second knight : crosses argent, on a field nondescript. (? Fitzurse ; suggests a garbled version of the usual Moreville coat.)

---

[1] R. Koechlin, *Les ivoires gothiques français*, 1929, Vol. II, No. 529 *ter.*

[2] R. Koechlin, *u.s.*, No. 346 *ter.*

[3] R. Koechlin, *u.s.*, No. 346 *bis.*

[4] I have to thank Miss M. H. Longhurst, F.S.A., for valuable information bearing on this category of work.

PLATE XXXI

1. ALABASTER TABLE, BRITISH
MUSEUM

FIFTEENTH CENTURY

2. IVORY PLAQUE, VICTORIA
AND ALBERT MUSEUM

FOURTEENTH CENTURY

3. LEAF OF IVORY DIPTYCH
VICTORIA AND ALBERT MUSEUM

FOURTEENTH CENTURY

4. LEAF OF IVORY DIPTYCH
LATE HOMBERG COLLECTION

FOURTEENTH CENTURY

PLATE XXXII

1. WOODCUT, WILLIAM CAXTON'S
GOLDEN LEGEND
1483

2. EMBROIDERED MITRE, MUNICH, BAVARIAN NATIONAL MUSEUM
FOURTEENTH CENTURY

Third knight : vert, semé of roundels sable. (? Moreville—compare the lost painting of St. John's, Winchester.)

The date of the glass is *c.* 1350, the arms of Edward III (1327–77) occurring in the window.

In the Stadtkirche (S. Dionys) of Esslingen, a stained-glass window to which reference has already been made in connexion with a single figure of St. Thomas Becket[1] also contains a rendering of the Martyrdom.

As to embroideries, I may briefly refer to the inclusion of the murder of St. Thomas among the subjects shown on some of the great examples of *opus anglicanum* —the copes in the Museo Civico at Bologna[2] and the Lateran,[3] and the dalmatic in the cathedral of Anagni[4] —as well as on the magnificent fifteenth-century chasuble in the possession of Stonyhurst College.[5] This scene was also at times embroidered on bishops' mitres, as may be seen from the fine example (Plate XXXII, fig. 2) in the Bavarian National Museum at Munich.[6] There are analogous mitres in the Treasury of the Sisters of Notre

[1] See *antea*, p. 32.

[2] Reproduced in L. de Farcy, *La Broderie*, Plate 27 (second numbering).

[3] Reproduced in L. de Farcy, *op. cit.*, Plate 43.

[4] Reproduced by Mrs. A. H. Christie, " A Reconstructed Embroidered Cope," in *The Burlington Magazine*, Vol. XLVIII (February 1926), p. 73.

[5] According to an inventory of 1388, the Vestry of Westminster Abbey in that year possessed an altar frontal embroidered with the Nativity, the Passion of St. Thomas Becket and the Life of St. Edward. The frontal is again mentioned in an inventory of 1540 : but by that time the St. Thomas subject had been removed from it. See J. Wickham Legg in *Archæologia*, Vol. LII (1890), p. 228, who suggests this may have been the famous frontal presented by Henry III in 1271.

[6] Already Dean Stanley (*Historical Memorials of Canterbury*, 7th ed., 1875, p. 230, n. 1) has drawn attention to the fact that here above the scene of the murder appears the hand of God between two crescents, and associates this circumstance with the presence of the famous gilded crescent in the roof of Canterbury Cathedral above the shrine of the saint.

Dame at Namur[1] and in the Cathedral Treasury at Sens.[2]

Of the category of woodcuts, which is plentifully made up chiefly from illustrations in editions of the *Golden Legend*, I will limit myself to reproducing one instance of definitely English interest, though of no great iconographical importance (Plate XXXI, fig. 1)—the woodcut which occupies the top of a page in Caxton's edition of the *Golden Legend* of 1483.[3]

I am passing somewhat rapidly over these examples, as the two principal categories associated with the representation of the martyrdom of St. Thomas Becket are the champlevé enamels and the paintings and these now demand to be treated of at some length.

The wide diffusion of relics of St. Thomas inevitably led to a corresponding demand for receptacles for these ; and this demand was, in a large measure, supplied by the Limoges enamellers of the thirteenth century.[4] The number of surviving Limoges châsses, either intact or

[1] See Joseph Braun in *Zeitschrift für Christliche Kunst*, Vol. XIX (1906), p. 291 *seqq.* (reproduction, p. 298).

[2] See E. Chartraire, *Inventaire du Trésor de l'Eglise primatiale de Sens* (Sens, 1897), p. 49. In the Sens mitre, as in the one at Munich, the other side shows the martyrdom of St. Stephen.

[3] Without attempting to give anything like a complete list, a few other examples of woodcuts of the Martyrdom in editions of the *Golden Legend* may here be mentioned : Lyons edition, 1483 and 1484, fol. c7v and fol. c6v respectively (scene out of doors, one murderer) ; *Der Heiligen Leben*, Strassburg, 1517, illustrations by Hans Baldung and Urs Graf, Vol. II, fol. 118 (scene out of doors, one murderer) ; *Legendario delle vite de'santi*, Venice, 1592, p. 79 (scene in church, two warriors in classical armour attacking St. Thomas, two of whose friends are present).

In *printed* Books of Hours an image of St. Thomas Becket, not a representation of the Martyrdom, is the rule (e.g. Hours, use of Sarum, Paris, 1526, fol. 12 v ; Paris, 1527, fol. 20 r).

[4] Of other reliquaries connected with St. Thomas Becket we may here note that containing a relic of the Saint's arm and hence shaped as an arm, in silver, which used to be in the cathedral of Gravina in the south of Italy, near Bari (cf. P. Ughelli, *Italia Sacra*,

more or less broken up, containing on the face a representation of the martyrdom of St. Thomas, is very large—larger than that of the châsses connected with any other saint—and they can be traced throughout the length and breadth of Europe, from Sweden in the north to the kingdom of the two Sicilies in the south. The Limoges châsses devoted to St. Thomas all date from the thirteenth century : at least I know of no examples dating from the twelfth century, and the series breaks off abruptly in the fourteenth. In that respect the St. Thomas châsses are, however, not peculiar, for the sudden extinction of the species of Limoges châsses in the fourteenth century is one of the most curious and inexplicable episodes of the history of mediæval art. The scene of the murder of Becket lent itself well to the frieze-like treatment which was the natural one for the shape of the caskets, and which made another subject—the journey and adoration of the Magi—such a very popular one for the Limoges châsses. As regards the treatment of the scene, it is a notable fact that an axe not infrequently figures among the equipment of the assailants, contrary to what is the case in most representations of the murder[1] : for the rest, there is a number of variations in the treatment of the scene, and on the whole very little heed was paid to anything like historical accuracy. The altar with the chalice placed on it is thus very seldom absent ; and on the other hand it is but very rarely that we find any indication of Grim or the other

1717, Vol. VII, col. 117). I have to thank Mr. A. Hamilton Smith, C.B., F.S.A., for this reference, as well as for a photograph of the comparatively recent reliquary which now replaces the old one at Gravina.

[1] In the relief on the Heidal reliquary (see *antea*, p. 76) and in one of the Norwich bosses, representing the Martyrdom, one of the knights carries an axe (see *antea*, p. 65) ; also in the Burlingham wall-painting the knight indicated by his coat-of-arms as Fitzurse, holds an axe with a long handle (see *postea*, p. 101).

friends of the archbishop. In this connexion the scenes
represented on four châsses demand to be investigated
closely. For one thing, the Cathedral Treasure at Sens
contains a châsse (Plate XXXIII, fig. 1)—made up
in the last century from different sources—the front of
which shows the martyrdom of a bishop, who has been
thought to be St. Thomas Becket and who is accompanied by two laymen who are being massacred by the
four assailants. The general disposition of the scene well
accords with that which we find in most martyrdoms of
St. Thomas on Limoges châsses. The altar with the
chalice is there, the Hand of God emerges from a cloud
above on the right, blessing the martyr ; and the axe
figures prominently among the weapons of the assailants.
Above, on the roof of the châsse, is, as may frequently
be paralleled, a symmetrical representation of the burial
of the martyr ; and the analogy of this arrangement
with the top portion of the Chartres window is one that
leaps to the eye. All things considered, in spite of the
undoubted analogies here displayed to the St. Thomas
Becket châsses, there is, however, every probability that
M. Mayeux[1] has found the right solution when inter-
preting the scene on the Sens châsse as relating to the
legend of St. Savinianus, a martyr of local renown in Sens,
who was slain together with two companions. Then there
is the very interesting case of the superb châsse (Plate
XXXIV), offered for sale by Major H. Chase Meredith
at Messrs. Sotheby's on July 17, 1930, and subsequently
acquired by the late M. Daguerre of Paris. This châsse
was published as far back as 1748 by Dr. Stukeley in
the *Philosophical Transactions* of the Royal Society ; and
at that time belonged to Sir John Cotton, to whom it
is surmised to have passed from a Mr. Eyre, of St. Neots,
who had discovered it in a house of that neighbourhood.

[1] See *Bulletin de la Société Nationale des Antiquaires de France*, 1923,
pp. 140–5, 151–3.

PLATE XXXIII

1. SENS CATHEDRAL

2. LONDON, SOCIETY OF ANTIQUARIES

ENAMELLED CHÂSSES
LIMOGES, THIRTEENTH CENTURY

PLATE XXXIV

ENAMELLED CHÂSSE
FORMERLY IN THE POSSESSION OF MAJOR H. CHASE MEREDITH

Dr. Stukeley puts forward the theory that it originally belonged to Croyland Abbey, in Lincolnshire, but of this there is no proof positive—the same provenance, by the way, has been attributed to a contemporary Limoges châsse in the British Museum, showing an undoubted representation of the Martyrdom of St. Thomas. On the front of the Meredith casket we see, below, a bishop who, officiating at an altar, is being attacked by three men coming from the left (one of them armed with an axe) while on the other side of the altar two monks stand witnessing the scene. On the roof, the story is continued by two scenes—on the left the burial of the martyr, and on the right angels carrying his soul to Heaven. In their general lines the scenes correspond very well with those occurring on numerous châsses illustrating the final scenes of the story of St. Thomas Becket. While admitting the possibility that the Meredith châsse may be connected with St. Thomas Becket, the presence of the two monks makes me personally incline to the view that Dr. Stukeley was right in identifying the principal martyr with Abbot Theodore, murdered by the Danes at the high altar of Croyland in 870, and the two monks with Friars Elfget and Savin, who were put to death on the same occasion. Thirdly, there is the case of a châsse which formerly was in the collection at the château of Goluchów and is only known to me from the description of it given by M. Molinier in his catalogue of the Goluchów collection.[1] The front of this châsse shows a saint, in episcopal vestments, standing at an altar, attacked from behind by *one* man : while in M. Molinier's words " deux apôtres, faisant un geste d'horreur, sont figurés debout, à droite et à gauche de la scene principale." Here the scene may very possibly represent the Martyrdom of St. Thomas ; and

---

[1] *Collections du Château de Goluchów—Objets d'art du Moyen Age et de la Renaissance*, Paris (privately printed), 1903, No. 136, p. 36.

the same is true of a châsse in the church of Clarholz (Westphalia) where the front shows a bishop at an altar attacked from behind by two men (one armed with an axe), while on the right a figure in a long cloak is watching, making a gesture of horror.[1] It is conceivable that the absence of a reference to Grim in the office of St. Thomas's Day (based upon the account by John of Salisbury) caused the omission of Grim in the representations of the murder on the Limoges châsses generally.

The only instance known to me of a châsse, the front of which shows a scene identifiable with the murder of St. Thomas Becket and including four assailants, is the noble casket belonging to the Society of Antiquaries (Plate XXXIII, fig. 2). Its provenance is Naples, where it was acquired by Sir William Hamilton in 1801, and the roof shows the burial of St. Thomas Becket. Much the largest groups among the material we are now surveying are those formed by châsses with fronts showing three or two assailants.

The following is a list of Limoges châsses known to me containing representations of the martyrdom of St. Thomas Becket in which *three* assailants appear :

Guéret Museum.[2]

Hereford Cathedral Library (Plate XXXV, fig. 1).

Liverpool Museum.

London, British Museum (front only).

Lyons Museum (from the E. Odiot collection) (Plate XXXVI, fig. 1).

Paris, late Schevitch collection (sale, Paris, 1910, no. 185).

Paris, late Spitzer collection, no. 236.

Trönö Church (Sweden) (Plate XXXV, fig. 2).

Utrecht, Archiepiscopal Museum, no. 907.

Zurich, Alfred Rütschi collection (sale at Lucerne,

---

[1] Reproduced in A. Ludorff, *Bau- und Kunstdenkmäler von Westfalen, Kreis Wiedenbrück* (Münster, 1901), Plate 3.

[2] Reproduced in E. Rupin, *L'œuvre de Limoges*, Paris, 1890, Plate XXXVIII.

Galerie Fischer, September 5, 1931, no. 31) ; from the Trivulzio collection.[1]

In the following examples *two* murderers occur :

Berlin, Schlossmuseum.

Clarholz Church.

Clermont Museum.

Escorial.[2]

Evreux, Doil collection.[3]

Hamburg, Museum für Kunst und Gewerbe (from the Bernal, Napier and Johannes Paul collections).

Limoges, Madame Fayette.[4]

London, British Museum : (1) Châsse surmised to have come from Croyland Abbey (Plate XXXVI, fig. 2) ; (2) Châsse, purchased 1854.

London, Victoria and Albert Museum, front of châsse (4041–1856).

London, Mr. Leopold Hirsch.[5]

Munich, A. S. Drey.

New York, Metropolitan Museum of Art.

Paris, Louvre, Donation Corroyer.

Paris, M. J. J. Marquet de Vasselot (from the collection of M. Martin le Roy).[6]

Paris, late Schevitch collection (sale 1910, no. 188).

Paris, late Tollin collection, 1897, front of châsse, no. 51.[7]

---

[1] Reproduced in the Sale catalogue.
[2] Reproduced in *Revue de l'Art Chrétien*, 1903, p. 299.
[3] Rupin, *op. cit.*, p. 426.   [4] *Ibid.*
[5] This châsse has an interesting provenance, being identical with one which once was in the collection of Horace Walpole at Strawberry Hill. A rough sketch of the latter is given in William Cole's manuscript collections in the British Museum (add. MSS. 5481, Vol. XL, p. 77). Cole also notes in *Journal of My Journey to Paris in* 1765, p. 151, in the church of St. Thomas du Louvre " a shrine on the wall " resembling the one at Strawberry Hill. What has become of the Paris châsse is not known.
[6] Reproduced in Vol. I, Plate XIX, of the illustrated catalogue of the Martin le Roy collection, No. 23.
[7] Reproduced p. 20 of the sale catalogue.

Paris, late R. . . . collection (sale June 12–13, 1924, nos. 49 and 50).[1]

Schloss Rohoncz collection (previously Vienna, Weinberger collection, sale October 24, 1929,[2] and prior to that in the cathedral of Palencia).

Rome, Treasure of the Lateran.[3]

Sigmaringen, late Hohenzollern collection.

Zurich, A. Rütschi collection (sold at Lucerne, September 5, 1931, no. 23)[4] ; from the Cardon collection.

Of the caskets with fronts containing three assailants, one is of particular interest since it forms part of the only châsse with a rendering of the murder of Becket which is now in English ecclesiastical ownership, belonging as it does to Hereford Cathedral (Plate XXXV, fig. 1). Another kindred example, to judge by the style of considerably later date, is in the possession of the church of Trönö in Sweden (Plate XXXV, g. 2). The examples next reproduced introduce us to a new type, inasmuch as the roof of the casket shows, not the actual entombment, but the soul of the deceased carried heavenwards in a halo by two angels. One example in which the assailants are three is in the Museum at Lyons (Plate XXXVI, fig. 1) ; another, which shows but two assailants, is

[1] The latter reproduced in the sale catalogue.

[2] Reproduced in the sale catalogue and in the catalogue of the Schloss Rohoncz collection, Exhibition at Munich, 1930, Plate 17.

[3] Reproduced in *Bollettino d'arte*, Vol. III, 1909, p. 32.

[4] Reproduced in the sale catalogue.

I have notes of the existence of châsses said to contain fronts representing the Martyrdom of St. Thomas Becket in the following collections, no details being available as to the number of assailants represented : Anagni Cathedral Treasure (Rupin) ; late Ducatel collection (Rupin) ; Sir Philip de M. Grey Egerton, Bart., exhibited at South Kensington, 1862, No. 1077, found near Tarporley in Cheshire.

PLATE XXXV

1. HEREFORD CATHEDRAL

2. TRÖNÖ, SWEDEN

ENAMELLED CHÂSSES

LIMOGES, THIRTEENTH CENTURY

PLATE XXXVI

1. LYONS MUSEUM   2. BRITISH MUSEUM

3. PARIS, MUSÉE DE CLUNY

ENAMELLED CHÂSSES
LIMOGES, THIRTEENTH CENTURY

now in the British Museum (Plate XXXVI, fig. 2), and as noted above is said originally to have had an English provenance and to have belonged to Croyland Abbey, Lincolnshire.

Finally, we have to note the type of which I know but two instances, the châsse just referred to at Goluchów and the one here reproduced at St. Laurent de Vigean, Mauriac, Cantal : here there is but one assailant, and above are seen the angels with the soul of the dead, whilst at the back is the burial scene.[1]

A further degeneration of the subject, iconographically speaking, might conceivably be the one seen on a châsse

Enamelled Châsse, St. Laurent de Vigean.

in the Musée de Cluny (Plate XXXVI, fig. 3), in which the slayers are two, but in which neither the setting of the scene nor the costume of the martyr points at all definitely to St. Thomas Becket. Still, as the scene has a vague relation to the murder of Becket and is accompanied by a burial scene on familiar lines, there is some excuse for the suggestion that St. Thomas Becket is the saint represented. On the other hand, there is also, for instance, the martyrdom of St. Candidus, slain by two soldiers, as represented on the eleventh-century reliquary in repoussé silver at S. Maurice d'Agaune : and the

[1] The châsse is here illustrated from the outline reproduction in Rupin, *op. cit.*, p. 397.

balance of probability is that either he or indeed some other saint than Becket is the martyr represented in the Cluny châsse.[1]

Of the paintings representing the murder of St. Thomas Becket, the illuminations form a group of great extent numerically, and also include a number of examples of great importance artistically. The earliest of these—dating from about 1190–1200—occurs in a psalter in the British Museum (Harl. 5102). It is an impressively silhouetted and strikingly dramatic composition which has been frequently reproduced, thereby becoming, as it deserves to be, a classic of the iconography of this subject (Plate XXXVII, fig. 1). The knights are four, Fitzurse being distinguished by his armorial bearings, a bear rampant : Grim is present holding the cross-staff, and the cap of the archbishop is shown falling to the ground. Also it will be noticed that there is no suggestion that the archbishop has been saying Mass. The illumination is accompanied by an almost equally finely designed rendering of the burial of St. Thomas.[2] Of about the same time as this psalter is the MS. known as the Huntingfield Psalter in the J. P. Morgan Library in New York, which contains an illumination of the Murder, in which four knights attack St. Thomas kneeling at an altar, one of the assailants wounding the archbishop in the head with his sword : behind the altar is seen Grim, holding the cross. A good deal later (c. 1233–50) is the illumination in the Carrow Psalter (Plate XXXVII, fig. 2), which used to be in the

[1] The scene of St. Valeria, beheaded and presenting her head to St. Martialis standing by an altar, which is a frequent subject on Limoges châsses, has at times been confused with the Martyrdom of St. Thomas Becket : as, for instance, in the interpretation of the châsse at Wartburg (Georg Voss, *Die Wartburg*, Jena, 1917, plate facing p. 278).

[2] Reproduced in Dom A. L'Huillier, *Saint Thomas de Cantorbéry*, Paris, 1891–92, Vol. II, plate facing p. 385.

PLATE XXXVII

1. BRITISH MUSEUM, HARL. 5102
1190–1200

2. CARROW PSALTER
C. 1233–50

ILLUMINATIONS, ENGLISH

PLATE XXXVIII

1. PANEL PICTURE, CANTER-
BURY CATHEDRAL
ENGLISH

FIFTEENTH CENTURY

2. PANEL PICTURE, STUTTGART
SUABIAN SCHOOL

C. 1520

3. ILLUMINATION, LUTTRELL PSALTER, ENGLISH

C. 1340

collection of the late Mr. Yates Thompson, a scene of even greater animation, introducing the trampling on the body of the martyr, which most accounts of the murder, as a matter of fact, associate with the degraded clerk who accompanied the slayers, Hugh of Horsea ; and as a notable rendering of about the same time we may further notice the tinted pen-and-ink drawing in Matthew Paris's *Historia Maior* in Corpus Christi College, Cambridge.[1] As time went by, the number of illuminations of this subject grew considerably, especially in Books of Hours, and the increasing realism was not invariably accompanied by proportionate historical accuracy. Reproductions are here given (Plate XXXVIII, fig. 3) of the vivid marginal illumination of this scene in the Luttrell Psalter (East Anglian, *c.* 1340) and of a couple of characteristic late renderings (Plate XXXIX)—each taken from a manuscript in the British Museum, Add. 17012 and King's 9—which serve to emphasize the strangeness of the absence of this subject among Flemish fifteenth- and sixteenth-century panel pictures. In Italian illuminations the scene can also be traced : I may quote the curious rendering,[2] by a possibly Umbrian miniaturist of the time about 1450, which occurs in an initial S in the collection of Signor Ulrico Hoepli of Milan : there is only one assailant, striking St. Thomas on the head with his sword ; the archbishop stands at an altar in the act of celebrating Mass ; on the left stands an acolyte holding a long candle.[3]

[1] For a reproduction of this see M. R. James, " The Drawings of Matthew Paris," in the Walpole Society's fourteenth volume, 1926, Plate III.

[2] Reproduced in Pietro Toesca, *Monumenti e Studi per la Storia della Miniatura italiana. La Collezione di Ulrico Hoepli*, Milan, 1930, Plate LXX.

[3] I am not attempting to give a census of illuminations representing the Martyrdom of St. Thomas Becket—a somewhat pointless undertaking. An index to those existing in the MSS. of the British

As to individual panel pictures of this subject the most notable existing example is an English picture (Plate XXXVIII, fig. 1)—the grievously injured one in Canterbury Cathedral at the head of the monument of Henry IV and Joan of Navarre,[1] dating from the second half of the fifteenth century. An interesting detail in the composition here is that the cap of St. Thomas, dashed off by the sword of one of his assailants (Fitzurse ?), lies on the floor.

The tabards worn by the knights in this picture are emblazoned thus : (1) Knight plunging his sword straight into St. Thomas's skull : three bears passant (Fitzurse) ; (2) Knight striking St. Thomas's head with his sword : three bears' heads muzzled (Le Bret) ; (3) Knight raising his sword to strike St. Thomas : or, two bars gules (de Tracy ; also shown on his shield) ; (4) Knight in the foreground, standing with his sword in its sheath and inactive : fretty, a fleur-de-lis in each fret (de Moreville).

A very curious rendering of the murder is that which occurs on the back of the rood-screen at Buckland-in-the-Moor, Devonshire. The panels, painted in grey monochrome as a continuous composition, are six in number, each with a single figure : those in the centre being St. Thomas, bleeding from a wound in his scalp, facing a figure, unarmed, but raising his right hand as if in derision (Plate XL). On the extreme left of the screen

Museum in 1879 is printed by W. de Gray Birch and H. Jenner in their book *Early Drawings and Illuminations*, p. 281 ; while those occuring in Books of Hours in the Bibliothèque Nationale in Paris have been noted by the Abbé V. Leroquais (*Les livres d'heures manuscrits de la Bibliothèque Nationale*, Paris, 1927, *a.l.*)

[1] Reproduced (in reconstruction) by J. Carter, *Specimens of Ancient Sculpture and Painting now remaining in England*, Vol. I, 1786, pp. 56–7. Carter's original water-colour, and also one of the actual condition of the panel, are in the Victoria and Albert Museum. Lately a very fine copy of the picture has been made by Prof. E. W. Tristram, which he kindly allows me to reproduce.

PLATE XXXIX

2. BRITISH MUSEUM, KING'S 9

ILLUMINATIONS, FLEMISH

C. 1500

I. BRITISH MUSEUM, ADD. 17012

PLATE XL

PAINTINGS ON ROOD-SCREEN, BUCKLAND-IN-THE-MOOR,
DEVONSHIRE, ENGLISH
EARLY SIXTEENTH CENTURY

is a man, holding a halberd, and next to him another, with a turban-like head-dress ; at the extreme right a figure in supplication and next to him a bald-headed man, indicated as a king (Henry II ?) by his ermine cloak. The figures have in parts been much injured, and the details of the scheme are difficult to interpret : in style, the paintings are undoubtedly very crude and caricature-like, but at the same time full of character, translating, as it were, the events of the Martyrdom into the terms of a popular Mystery Play. These panels date from the early sixteenth century.[1]

An interesting rendering of the murder is that which occurs on a narrow panel painted by an anonymous but capable Suabian master of about 1510–20, now in the ducal *Rentkammer* in Stuttgart (Plate XXXVIII, fig. 2). The saint kneeling in a church, with his mitre and crozier on the floor, is being slain from behind by one man, while in the distance a few spectators are seen. The panel has as its companion piece a picture, showing in the foreground a haloed youth kneeling, receiving the Host from a white dove, while further back he is disputing with four scholars. The inscription on the halo of the figure indicates the youth as being St. Edmund Rich, Archbishop of Canterbury, 1233–1240, and eventually, like St. Thomas Becket a refugee at Pontigny where his memory is still held in great veneration. If that identification be correct, the juxtaposition of the two saints would indeed be most interesting : and the words " SANCTVS EMVNDVS " do appear most plainly on the halo of the principal figure, though they are followed by the initials O.P., indicative of membership of the Dominican Order to which St. Edmund did not belong.

---

[1] The interpretation of these panels as illustrating the Murder of St. Thomas is due to Miss Rosemary Allan and Miss Audrey Baker and was made by them during an archæological expedition undertaken in the summer of 1931.

I think it, however, all things considered, most likely that these letters are the result of re-painting, and that hence in this Stuttgart picture we may recognize one of the very few existing items towards the iconography of St. Thomas's scholarly and ascetic successor in the reign of Henry III.[1] The selection of the subjects probably points to an influence from French Cistercian quarters, just as an inspiration from French sources has been recognized in the iconography of the great stained-glass window in the church of St. Denys at Esslingen in Suabia to which I have already had occasion to refer.

Of wall-paintings again, solely depicting the murder, there still exist a great many, and perhaps the earliest in the series is one not in England but in Italy, in the church of SS. Giovanni e Paolo at Spoleto (Plate XLI, fig. 1). As this fresco is closely akin in style to the work of a master, Alberto Sotio, who dated the crucifix in Spoleto Cathedral in 1187 or 1188, it is in all probability a work of the twelfth century. The fresco has been mutilated and is also in part covered up by later additions, but as far as can be made out it showed Henry II seated on the left, issuing his orders to the knights, the foremost of whom seizes by the hand St. Thomas, standing under a small edifice accompanied by Grim, and receiving the blow of the sword on his head. I am not acquainted with any other mediæval wall-paintings of this scene in Italy,[2] and with no existing one in

---

[1] I have to thank Graf Baudissin for a photograph of these pictures which in 1912–31 were exhibited in the Stuttgart Gallery (Nos. 103 e and f).

[2] It may be noted that the Martyrdom of St. Thomas bears a considerable resemblance to the Martyrdom of St. Magnus, as represented for instance in the fresco in the crypt in the cathedral of Anagni (reproduced by Toesca, loc. cit., Plate VII, facing p. 160); and to the death of St. Matthew as depicted, e.g. by Niccolò Pietro Gerini in the church of San Francesco at Prato (see R. van Marle,

PLATE XLI

1. FRESCO, SS. GIOVANNI E PAOLO, SPOLETO

LATE TWELFTH CENTURY

2. WALL-PAINTING, BURLINGHAM, ST. EDMUND

C. 1400

PLATE XLII

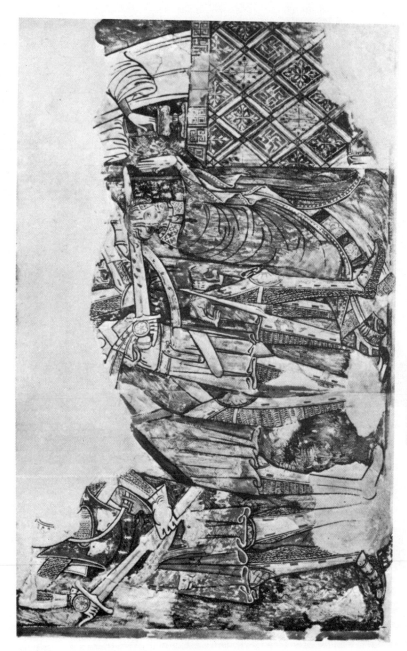

WALL-PAINTING, SOUTH NEWINGTON
C. 1350

France,[1] if we except the largely reconstructed rendering of the subject in one of the quadrilobes of the arcades of the upper church of the Sainte Chapelle in Paris. In the Rhineland one might expect to find some paintings of the subject, in view of the artistic and other relations between that part of Germany and England during the Middle Ages, but Professor Clemen, the foremost specialist on mediæval painting in the Rhineland, tells me that not a single specimen of the scene exists there.

In the church of St. Laurence at Lorch in Lower Austria, it has been thought that among the numerous scenes of martyrdom depicted in the first half of the fourteenth century on the wall of the *Marienkapelle*, the Murder of St. Thomas Becket has also found a place. These paintings have gone so faint and the composition in question is so fragmentary that it is difficult to be sure on this point : what is left shows a haloed figure standing at an altar, attacked from behind by a man with a sword.[2]

Turning then to England, we find that definite records exist of wall-paintings, certainly or possibly, of the murder of Becket, either lost or extant, to a number of

The Development of the Italian Schools of Painting, Vol. III, 1924, Fig. 350). Various handbooks repeat the statement, that a painting of the Martyrdom is to be seen in the church of San Tommaso Cantuariense at Verona, founded in 1316. This is, however, not now the case, as has been specially verified for me by my friend Marchese Alessandro da Lisca, who extended his researches to the adjoining barracks.

[1] G. B. Cola (*op. cit.*, p. 145) notes that a painting of the Martyrdom was to be seen in the church of St. Nicolas-sur-les-fossés at Arras, near the altar at which St. Thomas celebrated Mass in 1164. The church was pulled down in 1564. The treasury of Arras Cathedral contains the blood-stained rochet worn by St. Thomas Becket when he was slain.

[2] For reproductions see *Mitteilungen der K. K. Zentral-Kommission*, Ser. III, Vol. II (1903), p. 271 ; and compare F. Reichmann, *Gotische Wandmalerei in Niederösterreich*, Vienna, 1925.

between twenty and thirty ; and naturally the number was vastly greater before 1538.

The following is a survey of the iconographical material bearing on the Martyrdom alone, supplied by English wall-paintings known to the present writer :

Bramley, Hants (Plate XLIII, fig. 1), late thirteenth century.[1]

Burgh St. Peter, Norfolk, subject uncertain, destroyed.[2]

Burlingham St. Edmund, Norfolk (Plate XLI, fig. 2), fifteenth century.[3]

Canterbury, Eastbridge Hospital, now very fragmentary.[4]

Easton, Norfolk, fourteenth century.[5]

Eaton, Norfolk, fifteenth century.[6]

Faversham, Kent, concealed.[7]

Hemblington, Norfolk, All Saints, fragmentary, c. 1500.[8]

Hingham, Norfolk, concealed.[9]

Icklesham, Sussex, fragmentary.[10]

Lydiard Tregoze, Wilts, fifteenth century.[11]

Mentmore, Bucks, concealed.[12]

Newington (South), Oxon, fragmentary (Plate XLII), fourteenth century.[13]

Pickering, Yorks, St. Peter's (Plate XLIII, fig. 2), c. 1450.[14]

Preston, Sussex, damaged by fire in 1906, thirteenth century.[15]

---

[1] See *postea*, p. 99.   [2] Keyser, *List, ad litt.*

[3] See *postea*, p. 101.   [4] Keyser, *List*.   [5] *Ibid.*

[6] *Ibid.* ; reproduced in *Norfolk Archæology*, plate facing p. 165.

[7] Keyser, *List*.

[8] Communication from Miss Monica Bardswell.

[9] Keyser, *List*.

[10] *Sussex Archæological Collections*, Vol. XLIII (1900), p. 237.

[11] C. E. Ponting in *The Wiltshire Archæological and Natural History Magazine*, Vol. XXVII, 1911–12, p. 441. Now very much faded ; the mitre of St. Thomas seen on the floor as at Burlingham and Eaton.   [12] Keyser, *List*.

[13] Keyser, *Archæological Journal*, 1901, p. 54 ; and *postea*, p. 100.

[14] See *postea*, p. 101.

[15] Keyser, *List*, reproduced *Archæologia*, Vol. XXIII, Plate XXVI.

Stoke (North), Oxon, fourteenth century.[1]
Stone, Kent, thirteenth century.[2]
Stoneleigh, Warwick, destroyed.[3]
Stratford-on-Avon, Chapel of the Trinity, concealed, c. 1500.[4]
Sulhampstead Abbots, Berks.[5]
Upchurch, Kent, destroyed, subject uncertain.[6]
Wellow, Hants.[7]
Whaddon, Bucks, concealed.[8]
Winchester, St. John, destroyed, late thirteenth century (Plate XLIV, fig. 1).[9]
Winchester, Magdalen Hospital Chapel, subject uncertain.[10]
Winslow, Bucks, fifteenth century.[11]
Wootton Bassett, Wilts, destroyed.[12]
Yarmouth, Great, Norfolk, subject uncertain.[13]

Of existing examples, one of the finest, as well as earliest, is doubtless the painting in Bramley Church, Hants (Plate XLIII, fig. 1), which I am inclined to date towards the end of the thirteenth century. It is a most effective, dramatic composition, showing the delight which the painter evidently derived from the portrayal of the armour and the heraldic details ; whilst the delicacy in the painting of the head of St. Thomas is most

[1] Reproduced from a drawing by Prof. E. W. Tristram in F. Kendon, *Mural Paintings*, London, 1923.
[2] Tolerably well preserved ; drawing by Prof. Tristram at the church and Victoria and Albert Museum.
[3] Keyser, *List*.   [4] See *postea*, p. 101.
[5] Keyser, *Archæological Journal*, 1896, p. 176.
[6] Keyser, *List* (the interpretation mine).
[7] Keyser, *Archæological Journal*, 1896, p. 172.
[8] Keyser, *List*, reproduced in *Records of Buckinghamshire*, Vol. III (1863), plate facing p. 272.
[9] See *postea*, p. 100.   [10] Keyser, *List*.
[11] *Royal Commission on Historical Monuments (England)*, *Buckinghamshire*, Vol. II (1913), p. 341.
[12] Keyser, *List*.   [13] *Ibid.*

remarkable. As to the heraldry of the shields, we may here note that one of the lost paintings, that in the church of St. John at Winchester (Plate XLIV, fig. 1),[1] which has been dated about 1280–85, gave the blazons most accurately, viz. or, two bendlets gules (de Tracy) ; azure, fretty with a fleur-de-lis in each fret, argent (? Fitzurse—elsewhere this coat is given to Hugh de Moreville) ; argent, semé of crescents, pur (Le Bret) ; gules, semé of roundels, argent (de Moreville). There is, as a matter of fact, considerable variation in the heraldry in the different compositions ; and the usual charge for Fitzurse (occurring already in the illumination in the Psalter in the British Museum (Harl. 5102) and in the Bramley wall-painting) is a bear rampant. The painting formerly at St. John's, Winchester, is also notable in offering the only case known of a wall-painting showing the severed crown of St. Thomas's head falling to the ground : his cap, too, has been dashed off and much emphasis is laid on the fact that the four knights have entered the cathedral through the open door on the right.

Returning to existing examples, we must on no account pass over the wall-painting at South Newington, Oxon. The village is one in which a large number of miracles worked by St. Thomas occurred[2] : so little wonder that a particularly elaborate painting of the Martyrdom was done for the church.

The upper part of the composition (Plate XLII) is unfortunately gone : but what is left is very well preserved, and we can unmistakably make out from right to left, Grim, St. Thomas kneeling before the altar, and four knights, of which the third from the right is plunging

[1] Here reproduced from the illustration in *Journal of the British Archæological Association*, Vol. X, Plate 5.
[2] See Edwin E. Abbott, *St. Thomas of Canterbury*, London, 1898, Vol. I, p. 297 *seqq.*

PLATE XLIII

1. BRAMLEY CHURCH
LATE THIRTEENTH CENTURY

2. PICKERING CHURCH
FIFTEENTH CENTURY

WALL-PAINTINGS

PLATE XLIV

1. WALL-PAINTING (DESTROYED), ST. JOHN'S, WINCHESTER
THIRTEENTH CENTURY

2. WALL-PAINTING (DESTROYED), VENERABLE ENGLISH
COLLEGE, ROME, BY NICCOLÒ CIRCIGNANI
c. 1582

his sword into St. Thomas's skull. The knights carry
no visible shields : but the tabards over their armour
are prominently blazoned with heraldic charges, viz. :
first knight, a bear statant (Fitzurse) ; second knight,
a bend, possibly accompanied by crescents (Le Bret) ;
third knight, nothing visible ; fourth knight, several
dogs' heads erased. The whole is a splendid example of
English mid-fourteenth century painting ; and we are
particularly fortunate in having the head of St. Thomas
extremely well preserved.[1] Adjoining this subject is a
decapitation scene, which I do not think can have any
connexion with the St. Thomas Becket subject.

Of later date (*c.* 1400) is the painting in the church
of St. Edmund, Burlingham, Norfolk (Plate XLI, fig. 2),
a frieze-like composition of singular effectiveness and
monumental dignity : as to the heraldry, Le Bret now
carries a shield emblazoned with a bend engrailed
between two crescents, all within a bordure engrailed ;
while Fitzurse's shield has the bear rampant. The
latter also holds, as he should according to the authentic
accounts of the murder, an axe.[2]

Another very interesting example (*c.* 1450) showing a
variation on the usual type, is the painting in Pickering
Church, Yorks (Plate XLIII, fig. 2), in which are represented the four knights waiting before attacking Becket,
who is seen on the right kneeling in prayer. Of still later
examples known to us from reproductions, I may mention
the one in the chapel of the Trinity at Stratford-on-Avon,[3]

---

[1] I am extremely obliged to my friend Prof. E. W. Tristram
for allowing me to reproduce the splendid copy of this painting,
which he made after it recently had been cleaned.

[2] Both this wall-painting and the one at Bramley are reproduced
from water-colours kindly made for me by Mr. H. C. Whaite.
Closely allied in type to the Burlingham painting is the one at
Eaton (see above, p. 98).

[3] Reproduced in *A Series of Antient . . . Paintings . . . on the Walls
of the Chapel of the Trinity at Stratford-on-Avon*, 1836, Plate XIV.

which is an interior, carried out in the spirit of realism which we now, thanks to the rediscovery of the Eton wall-paintings, can associate with English wall-paintings of the late fifteenth century. In view of recent activities at Stratford one may hope that this wall-painting may yet be recoverable.

In later painting the subject is not a very frequent one. The tradition of depicting it was, however, kept up by the English College at Rome ;[1] it occurs in the series of gruesome scenes of martyrdom, painted about 1582, in the College, by Niccolò Circignani (il Pomarancio), and now only known from engravings—a series of which Monsieur Emile Mâle has appositely said, " L'histoire de l'Angleterre y était racontée presque uniquement par des supplices."[2]   The composition of the death of St. Thomas Becket (Plate XLIV, fig. 2) is, however, not a particularly harrowing one : it shows in the foreground the martyrdom, and in the distance on the left the council at Northampton, and on the right St. Thomas kneeling before Alexander III at Sens.[3]

Later again, we find an anonymous Italian artist of about 1700 representing the scene in a picture, still belonging to the College at Rome : the composition has

---

[1] Among the Latin plays composed probably in the seventeenth century for the students to act is The Tragedy of St. Thomas of Canterbury. Cardinal Gasquet, A History of the Venerable English College, Rome, London, 1920, p. 190 seq.

[2] See his article " Le martyre dans l'art de la Contre-Réforme " in Revue de Paris, February 15, 1929, p. 722.

[3] See the engraving by Giovanni Battista de Cavalieri (1525 ?–1601) in Ecclesiæ Anglicanæ Trophæa, Rome, 1584, Plate 24. In the foreground on the left also kneels a monk collecting with a shovel the blood and brains of St. Thomas which have formed a spring in the pavement, producing at times variously milk or blood, as the accompanying description sets out : Eius sanguis ac cerebrum in templi angulo projecti fontemque producunt ; qui semel in lac, quater in cruorem versus est. The office of the Day of St. Thomas (Lectio IX, In laudibus, 3rd Antiphone) refers also to this miracle.

here taken on a character strongly reminding us of renderings of similar subjects by Murillo, say his Martyrdom of St. Pedro Arbuez in the Hermitage.[1] Elsewhere in Italy, the Cremonese seventeenth-century painter Giovanni Battista Natali painted a picture of the martyrdom for the church of S. Pietro al Po in Cremona, where it still is. I am afraid I did not see it when visiting Cremona, but Mr. C. C. Oman describes it to me as showing " a Bossuet-like archbishop being murdered in a cathedral like that of Rennes." I have already previously noted[2] the presence, in the church of San Tommaso Cantuariense in Padua, of a picture of the Martyrdom by Giovanni Battista Pellizzari of Verona. While the church dedicated to St. Thomas Becket and founded as far back as about 1250, which formerly existed at Rovereto, contained a picture of the same subject by the Veronese painter Felice Boscaratti (1721–1807) now lost.

Again, in such a rare Roman Catholic publication as *The Life or the Ecclesiasticall Historie of S. Thomas, Archbishope of Canterbury*, printed at Cologne in 1639, there occurs a frontispiece with an engraving of the murder, signed " Huret inv. et f.," which shows a decidedly curious travesty of the subject into Baroque forms of peculiarly French Louis-Treize flavour : the artist is doubtless the celebrated French engraver Grégoire Huret (1606-1670).

Thanks to its interest in English mediæval history, fostered by the great French historians of the early

---

[1] Mr. Francis Shutt, of the Venerable English College, Rome, to whom I am indebted for photographs of this picture and the one by Durante Alberti, also kindly informs me that there exist records of a picture of St. Thomas by George Freman (?) painted in 1654, and of another painting for the church of the College in 1675 by Henry Corner (?)—English names evidently, though nothing is known about these artists, who were probably amateurs.

[2] See *antea*, p. 64.

nineteenth century, one would have imagined that the
Romantic school in France would have taken to this
subject with much zest ; one feels it ought to have
made a very congenial subject, say to Paul Delaroche,
but the nearest I have been able to get to him is a picture dated 1846, by one Camille Boucher, obviously an
artist who felt the influence of Delaroche.   The picture
alluded to hangs in the ambulatory of Sens Cathedral ;
and with a mention of it this survey of the iconography
of the Martyrdom of St. Thomas Becket may fittingly
come to a close.

CHAPTER V

THE ICONOGRAPHY OF HENRY II AND THE FOUR MURDERERS OF ST. THOMAS BECKET

A FEW subsidiary remarks bearing on the iconography of Henry II and the four knights may here not be out of place.
In the more elaborate series of scenes from the life of St. Thomas, Henry II, as we have seen, figures fairly often ; [1] and there are also cases in which he is brought into direct relationship with the murder. [2] Among the representations of scenes which occurred *after* the Martyrdom, the Penance of Henry II holds a most important place. The number of surviving examples is not inconsiderable, [3] and it may be assumed that after the issue of Henry VIII's edict against representations of St. Thomas, iconoclasm directed itself with particular zest against the subject showing the humiliation of Henry's namesake and predecessor on the throne of England. In this connexion we may also note the interesting suggestion made by Mr. Campbell Dodgson [4] that Dürer's woodcut of 1510, " The Penitent " (Bartsch 119) may represent Henry II doing penance before the

[1] Compare the illuminations of Queen Mary's Psalter and the Goethals-Danneel fragment ; the windows at Sens, Chartres and in the church of Saint Ouen at Rouen ; the wall-paintings at Brunswick ; the altarpiece at Wismar ; the alabaster table at Elham, Kent.

[2] E.g. in the bas-relief of the Lyngsjö font and the fresco in SS. Giovanni e Paolo at Spoleto.

[3] Compare the stained glass in the Bodleian Library, and in Checkley Church, Staffs, the Norwich bosses (twice), and the Tettens altarpiece. A pilgrim's sign in the London Museum should also be noted in this connexion.

[4] See *The Burlington Magazine*, Vol. LIII (October 1928), p. 203.

shrine of St. Thomas Becket. Unfortunately, however, there is nothing at all to indicate a kingly rank in Dürer's penitent : nor was Henry II's scourging on the occasion of his penance self-administered.

Few popular traditions of the Middle Ages are more fascinating than those which tell, with many variations and frequent contradictions, of the fate which overtook the four slayers of St. Thomas Becket : of the table at South Malling Manor, near Lewes, where the four repaired on December 31, which would continue to throw off their arms when these were placed on it ; of the fourteen years that Fitzurse, Le Bret and Moreville were sentenced by Pope Alexander III to spend on crusaders' service in the Holy Land, a period curtailed by their death to three years ; of Tracy, by the bulk of tradition indicated as the first to wound St. Thomas, and against whom and whose descendants the winds would always blow—" The Tracys—Have always the wind in their faces "—and many other picturesque episodes. It stands to reason that the iconography of the knights—apart from the representations of the murder and the episodes which immediately preceded it—cannot be an extensive one. In his celebrated dialogue *Peregrinatio Religionis Ergo* (first published in the enlarged edition of Erasmus's *Colloquies*, printed at Basle in 1524, and probably written in that year) Erasmus describes how he saw in the south porch of Canterbury Cathedral " stone statues of the three knights who with impious hands murdered the most holy man : their family names are inscribed, Tuscus, Fuscus and Berrus." The names, as reported by Erasmus, are doubtless corruptions of " Tracy," " Fitzurse " and " Le Bret " ; and it is interesting to note that Moreville, as technically not a murderer, was not included in the series.[1] These

[1] It is a curious fact that Paulus Hentzner in his *Itinerarium Germaniæ, Galliæ, Angliæ, Italiæ* (Nuremberg, 1612), describing a

statues have vanished, though in the locality indicated by Erasmus there is still a sculptured crucifix between the figures of the Virgin and St. John and with fragments of a sword at its foot, indicating the " *altare ad punctum ensis* "—the broken sword of Richard Le Bret. On the question why these statues were set up, Erasmus offers some considerations in his characteristic caustic vein :

" *Menedemus.* Why is so much honour bestowed on the impious ?

Ogygius. The same degree of honour is bestowed upon them which is bestowed on Judas, Pilate, Caiphas and the band of wicked soldiers, which you see laboriously sculptured on golden altars. Their names are added, that the guilt of their crime should ever attach to them. They are thrust forward into sight, that no courtier should hereafter lay his hands upon bishops, or upon the property of the church. For those three courtiers, after the perpetration of their crime, were seized with madness, nor were they restored to reason until the intercession of the most holy Thomas had been implored.

Menedemus. Oh the unfailing clemency of the martyrs ! "[1]

One may surmise that considerations similar to those which prompted the setting up of these statues at Canterbury were the *raison d'être* of the curious stained-glass window which still in the early seventeenth century was

visit to England in 1598 and mentioning these effigies, gives the names exactly as Erasmus (the genitive forms " Tusci," " Fusci " and " Berri " being used in both instances). If the statues really remained intact in the days of Queen Elizabeth, it would be a quaint and significant illustration of the moral revaluation of the action of the three knights.

[1] See J. G. Nichols, *Pilgrimages to Saint Mary of Walsingham and Saint Thomas of Canterbury*, Westminster, 1849, p. 45 *seq.*

to be seen in the church of Brereton in Cheshire. The
window was tripartite and in two tiers, the main one
containing, under canopies, figures of the four knights,
with drawn swords, each named by a scroll, standing
on either side of a figure in armour, also with drawn
sword, holding a scroll inscribed " Martirium Thomae."
Above were three figures, one, doubtless St. Thomas
Becket, in the centre and two others, less certain of
identification, at the sides.[1]

Finally, we may recall the Stoke d'Abernon wall-
painting, showing St. Thomas with a man in armour,
perhaps one of the knights kneeling before him, to which
reference was made above[2]—a work the expiatory sig-
nificance of which if not a certainty is at least a considerable possibility.

Memorials of the special character of this painting
(if correctly interpreted) of the Brereton window and
the Canterbury effigies must, however, inevitably have
been rare. In the main, popular abhorrence of the
deed of the four slayers of St. Thomas found its
most graphic expression in the weird and vivid tales
about them which sprang from the inexhaustible
resources of popular imagination.

[1] An engraving of this window, from a drawing made in 1608,
may be seen in *Archæologia*, Vol. IX (1789), plate facing p. 368.

[2] See *antea*, p. 37.

APPENDIX I

ITEM FOR as moche as it appereth now clerely, that Thomas Becket, somtyme Archbyshop of Canturburie, stubburnely to withstand the holsome lawes establyshed agaynste the enormities of the clergie, by the kynges highnes mooste noble progenitour, kynge HENRY the seconde, for the common welthe, reste, and tranquillitie of this realme, of his frowarde mynde fledde the realme into Fraunce, and to the bishop of Rome, mayntenour of those enormities, to procure the abrogation of the sayd lawes, wherby arose moch trouble in this said realme, And that his dethe, whiche they vntruely called martyr-dome, happened vpon a reskewe by him made, and that, as it is written, he gaue opprobrious wordes to the gen-tyll men, whiche then counsayled hym to leaue his stub-bernesse, and to auoyde the commocion of the people, rysen up for that rescue. And he nat onely callyd the one of them bawde, but also toke Tracy by the bosome, and violently shoke and plucked hym in suche maner, that he had almoste ouerthrowen hym to the pauement of the churche, So that vpon this fray one of their company perceiuyinge the same, strake hym, and so in the thronge Becket was slayne, And further that his Canonization was made onely by the bysshop of Rome, bycause he had ben a champion to maynteyne his vsurped auctoritie, and a bearer of the iniquitie of the clergie, for these and for other great & vrgent causes, longe to recyte, the kynges maiestie, by the aduyse of his counsayle, hath thought expedyent, to declare to his louynge subiectes, that notwithstandynge the sayde canonization, there

appereth nothynge in his lyfe and exteriour conuersa-
tion, wherby he shuld be callyd a sainct, but rather
estemed to haue ben a rebell and traytour to his prynce :
Therfore his grace strayghtly chargeth and command-
eth, that from hense forth the sayde Thomas Becket shall
not be estemed, named, reputed, nor called a sayncte,
but bysshop Becket, and that his ymages and pictures,
through the hole realme, shall be putte downe and
auoyded out of all churches, chapelles, and other places,
and that from hense forthe, the dayes vsed to be festiuall
in his name, shall not be obserued, nor the seruice, office,
antiphones, collettes, and prayers in his name redde, but
rased and put out of all the bokes. And that all other
festiuall dayes, all redy . abrogate, shalbe in no wyse
solemnised, but his gracis ordynance and Iniunctions
thervpon obserued : to thentent his gracis louynge
subiectes shall be no lengar blyndely ledde and abused,
to cõmitte idolatrie, as they haue done in tymes passed,
vpon peyn of his maiesties indignation, & imprisonment
at his gracis plesure. FINALLY his maiestye wylleth,
and chargeth all his said trewe louynge and obedient
subiectes, that they and euery of them for his part, shall
kepe and obserue all and syngular the Iniunctions, made
by his maiestie, vppon the peyne therein conteyned, and
further to be punyshed at his graces pleasure.

GOD SAVE THE KYNGE

Vvestm̃. XVI Nouembr. Anno regni regis Henrici
octaui XXX.

Tho. Berthelet. regius impressor
excudebat

CVM PRIVILEGIO.

(From a copy of the Proclamation in the possession
of the Society of Antiquaries.)

APPENDIX II

ICONOCLASM DIRECTED AGAINST ST. THOMAS BECKET IN THE REIGN OF QUEEN MARY TUDOR

1554, Feb. 19. " Christofer Hunnyngwood suspected to have cutt of the hed of the ymage of S. Thomas, was committed to the Towre to be thier secretly kept without having Conference with any."

> (Privy Council Proceedings, Westminster ; Cod. Harl. 643, fol. 39b. See *Acts of the Privy Council of England*, N.S., vol. V (1892), p. 97 and *Archæologia*, vol. XVIII, p. 181.)

1555, March 14. " Vpon Thursedaye in yᵉ night, beynge yᵉ xiiii of Marche, yᵉ Image of a byshope, whiche was newly sett vp of late over yᵉ dore of sent Thomas of Acars, was shamefully mangled, yᵉ heade & yᵉ ryght arme beynge cleane smyttyn of : yᵉ whiche Image ones before this tyme had yᵉ hede lykewyse stryken of, and was aftarwarde newly set vp, and noue eft sones broken."

> (See " A London Chronicle 1523–1555 " ; *Camden Miscellany*, vol. XII, p. 42.)

" The 14 of Marche, about ix of the clock at night, an image of St. Thomas of Canterburie, which was new made in stone (by the commaundement of the King and Queenes Councell) by the wardens of the Mercers and sett over the Chappell doore of the Mercers hall and Churche in Cheape, was broken and defaced, but the auctor of that fact could not be heard of or fownd out, notwithstandinge a Proclamation made in that behalfe."

> (See Wriothesley's " Chronicle," *Camden Soc.*, vol. II, p. 127.)

APPENDIX III

SYNOPSIS OF SUBJECTS RELATING TO ST. THOMAS BECKET IN THE THIRTEENTH-CENTURY STAINED GLASS IN CANTERBURY CATHEDRAL

Trinity Chapel

North wall, third window (counting from the west). (1)–(2) Pilgrims proceeding to Canterbury. (3) A King (Henry II ?) in conversation with Benedict, chronicler of the miracles of St. Thomas Becket. (4) A Cure of St. Thomas.

North wall, fourth window. (1) Scene at the tomb. (2) St. Thomas curing a man in bed. (3) Scene comprising four women. (4) Incident in a cure. (5)–(8) Modern. (9)–(10) Cure of the diseased leg of Robert of Cricklade, Prior of St. Frideswide, Oxford. (11)–(12) Cure of a woman. (13)–(14) A lunatic restored to reason. (15)–(16) Scenes relating to the curative effect of holy water of Canterbury.

South wall, fifth window. (1) Apparition of St. Thomas, out of his shrine, to Benedict. (2)–(3) Two cures of diseased legs. (4) Cure of a sick man, presumably Godwine of Boxgrove. (5)–(6) Curing of two blind women. (7)–(9) Modern. (10)–(12) Cure of two lame women. (13)–(17) Story of Eilward of Westoning, whose eyes, put out as punishment, were restored by St. Thomas Becket. (18) Modern. (19)–(21) Story of the cure of the physician of Périgord, suffering from dropsy. (22) Modern.

South wall, sixth window. (1)–(3) Healing of a blind woman. (4)–(5) Incidents from the story of the Irish soldier Walter. (6) A sick man in bed waited upon by his mother. (7) Scene at the tomb. (8) Various figures in conversation. (9) Scene at the tomb. (10)–(12) Almost wholly modern. (13)–(15) Story of the boy

8

Robert, brought back to life after drowning in the Medway. (16)–(18) Modern. (19)–(21) Story of the insane woman, Matilda of Cologne. (22)–(24) Modern. (25)–(33) Story of the Knight Jordan, son of Eisulf, who was dilatory in fulfilling a vow to St. Thomas Becket.

SOUTH CHOIR AISLE

Triforium, first window (counting from the East). Two scenes from the story of the carpenter William of Kellett wounded in his leg and healed by St. Thomas. One scene from the story of John of Roxburgh saved from the Tweed.

Triforium, second window. Three scenes from the story of William of Kellett.

Triforium, third window. One scene from the story of William of Kellett ; one from that of Philip, son of Hugh Scott, restored to life after drowning ; and one from the story of John of Roxburgh.

GENERAL BIBLIOGRAPHY

ABBOTT (EDWIN A.), *St. Thomas of Canterbury, his Death and Miracles.* 2 vols. London, 1898.
Invaluable on account of its painstaking collation and criticism of the various accounts of the death of St. Thomas as well as for its synopsis of the miracles.

ARNOLD-FOSTER (FRANCES), *Studies in Church Dedications of England's Patron Saints.* 3 vols. London, 1899.
Particularly useful on account of its synopsis of the dedications of churches in England to St. Thomas Becket. In all, about eighty such dedications have so far been traced.

BOND (FRANCIS), *Dedications and Patron Saints of English Churches.* Oxford, 1914.

BORENIUS (TANCRED), " The Iconography of St. Thomas of Canterbury " in *Archæologia*, vol. LXXIX, pp. 29–54. London, 1929.

——" Addenda to the Iconography of St. Thomas of Canterbury " in *Archæologia*, vol. LXXXI, pp. 19–32. London, 1931.

HORSTMANN (C.), *The Early South English Legendary.* Early English Text Society, 1887.

HUTTON (W. H.), *Thomas Becket, Archbishop of Canterbury.* First edition, London, 1910. Second edition, Cambridge, 1926.
A masterly and compact study of the subject.

JUSSERAND (J. J.), *English Wayfaring Life in the Middle Ages (XIV century).* First edition, 1889. Second edition, 1920. Third edition, 1925.
In this classic on its subject, the pilgrimages to Canterbury are dealt with on pp. 348 *sqq.*

L'HUILLIER (DOM A.), *Saint Thomas de Cantorbéry.* 2 vols. Paris, 1891–92.
A work of the most solid learning ; a storehouse of information.

MAGNUSSON (EIRIKIR), *Thómas Saga Erkibyskups. A Life of Archbishop Thomas Becket in Icelandic with*

English Translations. 2 vols. London, 1875–83. (Master of the Rolls Series, No. 65.)

MEYER (PAUL), *Fragments d'une vie de Saint Thomas de Cantorbéry en vers accouplés.* Société des Anciens Textes français. Paris, 1885.

MORRIS (JOHN) S.J., *The Life and Martyrdom of Saint Thomas Becket,* Archbishop of Canterbury. First edition, London, 1859. Second edition, London, 1885.

NOTES AND QUERIES, Ser. X, vol. I, June 1, 1904, pp. 450–452 ; vol. II, July 9, 1904, pp. 30–32.

Symposium on the Iconography of St. Thomas Becket and on dedications to the Saint, in response to an enquiry by Mr. H. Snowden Ward.

ROBERTSON (JAMES CRAIGIE), *Materials for the History of Thomas Becket, Archbishop of Canterbury,* 7 vols. London, 1875–85. (Master of the Rolls Series, No. 67.)

A monumental work, indispensable to the student of the life and cult of St. Thomas Becket. Vol. 7 edited by J. B. Sheppard.

STANLEY (ARTHUR P.), *Historical Memorials of Canterbury.* London, numerous editions, the first in 1855. Quoted in this volume from the seventh edition, 1875.

Contains the two papers " The Murder of Becket " (enlarged from an article in the *Quarterly Review* for September 1853) and " The Shrine of St. Thomas of Canterbury," which are of fundamental importance to the study of all questions concerning St. Thomas Becket.

WALBERG (E.), " La Vie de Saint Thomas le Martyr par Guernes de Pont-Sainte-Maxence " ; in *Skrifter utgivna av Kungl. Humanistiska Vetenskapssamfundet i Lund.* Lund, 1922.

—— *La Tradition Hagiographique de Saint Thomas Becket avant la fin du XIIe siècle.* Paris, 1929.

WARD (H. SNOWDEN), *The Canterbury Pilgrimages.* First edition, London, 1904. Second edition, London, 1927.

Collates succinctly and pleasantly the information concerning the pilgrimages to Canterbury.

INDEX OF PLACES

117